THE HIDDEN HAND OF GOD

REMARKABLE ANSWERED PRAYERS

THE HIDDEN HAND OF GOD

REMARKABLE ANSWERED PRAYERS

Surely there are in everyone's life certain connections, twists and
turns which pass awhile under the category of Chance, but at
the last, well examined, prove to be the very hand of God.
—Sir Thomas Browne

CARMEL • NEW YORK 10512

www.guideposts.org

Acknowledgments

Every attempt has been made to credit the sources of copyrighted material used in this book. If any such acknowledgment has been inadvertently omitted or miscredited, receipt of such information would be appreciated.

Scripture marked (KJV) are taken from *The New Open Bible, Study Edition,* King James Version. Copyright © 1990 by Thomas Nelson, Inc.

Scripture marked (NIV) are taken from *The Holy Bible, New International Version.* Copyright © 1973, 1978, 1984 International Bible Society. Used by permission of Zondervan Bible Publishers.

Scripture marked (NKJV) are taken from *The Holy Bible*, New King James Version. Copyright © 1997, 1990, 1985, 1983 by Thomas Nelson, Inc.

Scripture marked (NRSV) are taken from the *Common Bible*, New Revised Standard Version Bible. Copyright © 1989 by the Division of Christian Education of the National Council of the Churches of Christ in the U.S.A. Used by permission. All rights reserved.

"A Perfect Mistake" copyright © 1998 by Cheryl Walterman Stewart. Used by permission of the author.

"A Place Prepared by God" copyright © 1993 by Catherine E. Verlenden. Used by permission of Catherine E. Verlenden.

"A Prayer for the Shepherd" by Mike Nappa is from *True Stories of Answered Prayer.* Copyright © 1999 by Nappaland Communication, Inc. Used by permission of Tyndale House Publishers. All rights reserved.

"A Special Friend" and "Unseen Hands" by Kelsey Tyler are from *It Must Have Been a Miracle.* Copyright © 1995 by Karen Kingsbury. Published by the Berkley Publishing Group.

"Another Sleepless Night" by Donna Weber, "Expect a Miracle, Mama" by Tina Coligan-Holt, and "Prayers for Elijah" by Azriela Jaffe are from *Mothers' Miracles,* compiled and edited by Jamie C. Miller, Laura Lewis, and Jennifer Basye Sander. Copyright © 1999 by Jamie C. Miller, Laura Lewis, and Jennifer Basye Sander. Published by William Morrow and Company, Inc.

"Behind Enemy Lines" (originally titled "Captain Scott O'Grady") copyright © 1997 by Walter L. Walker.

"Capsized!" by Debra Laughlin first appeared in *Today's Christian Woman* magazine (July/August 1999). Copyright © 1999 by Debra Laughlin. Used by permission of the author.

The Celtic prayer called "Lord, Save" is from *Tides and Seasons* by David Adam. Copyright © 1989 by David Adam. Published by Triangle/SPCK, London.

(continued on page 163)

THE HIDDEN HAND OF GOD

REMARKABLE ANSWERED PRAYERS

Prayer is a conversation of love. It is the sweet song of love, composed by the Creator of the universe, flowing from His wide heart to encompass each one of us. God seeks intimacy with us and prayer is the language of that intimacy, our means of communication and intimacy with the Holy God, the One Who loves us with the great heart of a father.

There are many kinds of prayer—worship, adoration, repentance, thanksgiving, supplication—all of which speak to the various aspects of a personal relationship with God. But probably the most dramatic prayers of all are petitions, those prayers in which we ask God to intercede in our lives in very specific ways. Petitions are special in that these are occasions of particular need, when we storm the gates of heaven, as it were, to seek God's intervention in our lives in very unambiguous terms.

Sometimes we make the mistake of thinking that petitionary prayer is the only prayer. The only time we pray is when we find ourselves in distress or danger. This is akin to that family member who calls only when he needs money. While we're generally willing to help, we also grieve for the loss of the loving intimacy that could be part of the relationship. But there are also grave risks in not going to family when we're in need because we're too proud or too fearful.

Petitionary prayer fills the Bible. We are encouraged to ask God for help, for ordinary needs and for extraordinary needs. The Psalms are filled with petitions. And the stories of the Bible are replete with petitions for God's help and intervention in our lives. Jesus encourages us to ask. In his example of how to pray, he instructs us to ask God for our daily bread—for the most fundamental things in life. And another time he clearly encourages us to go to God with our needs:

> *"Ask, and it will be given you; search, and you will find; knock, and the door will be opened for you. For everyone who asks receives, and everyone who searches finds, and for everyone who knocks, the door will be opened. Is there anyone among you who, if your child asks for bread, will give a stone? Or if the child asks for a fish, will give a snake? If you then, who are evil, know how to give good gifts to your children, how much more will your Father in heaven give good things to those who ask him!" (Matthew 7:7–11, NRSV)*

Experience shows us that God is interested in every area of our lives. God participates in the everyday, providing our daily needs, aiding in the small things that make our lives more fulfilling and joy-filled, and in our work. He steps in when we find ourselves in danger or when our children need protection. And possibly the most thrilling experience of prayer is when we become agents of God by becoming intercessors, or even more exciting, becoming an answer to someone else's prayer.

Our experiences with prayer can vary vastly, from the common to the profound. Yet at every turn, we are aware of our link of love to the Creator made possible through this thing called prayer.

We never tire of hearing stories of God's great faithfulness to us, when He steps in to help us in our times of greatest need. Certainly stories of God's miraculous intervention fill television programs and bookstore shelves. And on the face of it, these stories may seem like simply a form of sacred entertainment: stories with great "ooo-aah" factors, and our response is "Wow." But in truth, inspiring stories of answered prayer are valuable because they teach us about God's love for us and can lead us more deeply into a life of prayer.

In recounting stories of God's answers to our prayers we follow a great tradition of remembering God's goodness to us. To "remember" in the Bible is not merely to recall to mind; it is to express concern for someone, to act with loving care for him. Consider for a moment our need to remember. Every aspect of our lives is defined and given meaning because we remember. This is why we value photographs and diaries, journals and genealogies, museums and ceremonies. Even our calendars, which we may think are meant for planning ahead, are actually designed to help us remember—the date of a parent's wedding, a child's birth, as well as dates important to our nation's life and the seasons that mark the rhythm of our religious lives.

As we read these stories, let's remember God's goodness, remember His faithfulness, remember His love for us as He hears us and responds in His love. For in remembering, we honor God and glorify Him.

> O my people, hear my teaching;
>> listen to the words of my mouth.
> I will open my mouth in parables,
>> I will utter hidden things, things from of old—
> what we have heard and known,
>> what our fathers have told us.
> We will not hide them from their children;
>> we will tell the next generation
> the praiseworthy deeds of the LORD,
>> his power, and the wonders he has done.

—Psalm 78:1–4 (NIV)

Enjoying God's Bounty
Prayers of Provision

Chapter 1 Gifts for Daily Living

Have you ever listened to a child pray? Trusting and unpretentious, children fill their prayers with the concerns and joys of everyday life: a new puppy, a sick teacher, a bully at school. These are elemental prayers that do not rely on sophisticated formulae or well-modulated voices. These are the prayers of daily life.

A child understands instinctively that a loving parent is pleased to hear his voice and even more, welcomes his company. When we approach God as His children, He happily responds, infusing himself into our lives, welcoming us into His presence. He *welcomes* us. It is such a profound gift!

What we discover also is that God is interested in our daily lives: not simply the dramatic events or defining moments of our lives, but the quiet moments, the times we call "ordinary" or "daily." It is in the daily that intimacy is found, and intimacy with His creation is God's greatest desire. He wants us to come to him with our daily needs, when we've lost something we cherish, when we need a special friend, or our family close by. These petitions are not petty or shallow or trivial. These are the simple requests that a child makes to a loving parent, in full confidence they will be answered, for the simple reason that a parent loves completely and without reservation.

As we read these stories of God's care, let's remember that we are His children, and that He wants us to know that He loves us.

How brief is our span of life compared with the time since you created the universe. How tiny we are compared with the enormity of your universe. How trivial are our concerns compared with the complexity of your universe. How stupid we are compared with the genius of your creation. Yet during every minute and every second of our lives you are present, within and around us. You give your whole and undivided attention to each and every one of us. Our concerns are your concerns. And you are infinitely patient with our stupidity. I thank you with all my heart—knowing that my thanks are worthless compared to your greatness.

—St. Fulbert of Chartres (960–1028)

"EXPECT A MIRACLE, MAMA"

TINA COLIGAN-HOLT

When I moved from a big city to a small town in Texas, I felt a little out of place. The residents of Pampa were down-home, simple country folk, and the one thing they were all proud of was the beautiful gardens in each of their backyards. In an attempt to join with my new community, I decided it was time to plant a garden of my own. This was a new endeavor for me, so when one of my neighbors recommended using compost, which I could get free from the city landfill, I decided to give it a try.

I loaded up our new van with my four children, a shovel, three buckets, and a plastic bag, and headed over to the landfill. As soon as I pulled up and opened my door, I was hit by a gust of wind, and one of my contact lenses flew out of my eye. I could think of only two things at that moment: one, that finding a contact in a compost pile had to be at least as difficult as finding a needle in a haystack, and two, that finding the hundred dollars for a new set of contacts and an eye exam might even be harder than that! Still determined to get the compost, however, I loaded it up, keeping my one eye closed so I could focus.

The events of the next hour made me wonder if I would ever measure up to my "green-thumbed" neighbors. I dragged the plastic bag full of compost into our yard, not knowing there was a hole in the bottom, and left a dirty trail from inside our new van all the way to the backyard. Eager to get the compost on my garden, I started putting it around every plant by hand. Naturally, one of the times I reached into the bucket, I picked up a big, squishy cow patty. Then as I stepped across one of the wooden planks outlining my beds, it skidded across the mud like a surfboard, and I fell flat into the garden doing the splits! As I sat in the mud, my frustration turned to hysteria and I began laughing uncontrollably. My children looked at me as though I had lost my mind, and I believe we were all feeling that it was time to head back to the big city.

Trying to divert all of our attention to something more constructive, I asked the children to help me search the van to see if the wind had blown my contact lens inside it somewhere. We searched the floorboards, the seats, the ashtray, every nook and cranny. We couldn't find it anywhere. I finally resigned myself to the fact that it was gone for good. Sensing my discouragement, each of my kids told me they were sorry we had had such a bad day. It certainly was one of the worst since our move. Maybe I was struggling too hard to fit into a town in which I really didn't belong. I was lonely—I missed my family and friends. Why had we moved here, anyway? Privately, I questioned God, asking what He was trying to tell me. I begged Him to make it known to me.

The night was over and I was tired. I went to each of my children to say good night. When I got to my nine-year-old son, Trey, he looked up at me and said,

"Mama, do you believe in miracles?" Not wanting to crush the faith of a child, I responded, "I sure do!" And he said, "Well, why haven't we had any miracles in our lives?"

I suddenly realized what a disservice I was doing to my children by sulking over something as trivial as a contact lens. So I proceeded to tell him some of the wonderful miracles and blessings we had received in our lives. Like the time he was a nine-month-old baby in Texas Children's Hospital with a hundred and six-degree temperature, and the doctors didn't know what was wrong. After a week of tests and observation, they determined that Trey probably had a birth defect that would require surgery. Before going in for a final test, I said a quick prayer, and off we went to the X-ray room. I held my little baby down during the X-rays, with tears streaming down my face. We went back into the room to wait for the results. The doctor came in smiling and said, "You got your miracle. No surgery will be necessary. Everything is working as it should. You can go home now." I explained to Trey that this was indeed a wonderful miracle, but he was just too young to remember it.

Then he said, "Mama, maybe if we pray to God, you'll get a miracle and find your contact lens." Of course. Such a simple solution to a child. Why did faith always seem so much more complicated to adults? Needing his strength, I said, "Will you pray with me?" So we did. Trey led us in a wonderful prayer straight from a child's innocent heart. Right afterward he turned to me and said, "Mama, did you check your purse?"

All of a sudden, I remembered that my purse had been sitting open by the driver's seat when I got out of the van at the compost pile. I ran to my bedroom to get my purse. Trey and I plopped down on the living room floor. We spread out a sheet to catch all of the articles as I dumped it out. My husband was lying on the couch after a hard day of work and looked over at us. Puzzled, he said, "What on earth are you doing?" I smiled at Trey and said, "We're finding my contact lens. We have reason to believe it's in here." I searched meticulously through the pile on the floor, but once again, I found no lens.

In a last-ditch effort, I picked up the empty purse and peeked inside. To my amazement, there it was on the bottom, safe and sound. Trey and I rejoiced at our miracle, and I immediately put it safely away in its case.

I was deeply touched by this very simple event that proved to me the power of a child's faith. So often, children are God's answer to our depression, discouragement and loneliness. But more than that, while we are busy teaching them how to be adults, they are teaching us how to be children. And the longer I live, the more I realize the strength of that quality—"to become as a little child."

Because of the example of a small child, my faith continues to grow and flourish. And incidentally, so does my garden.

INNOCENT PETITIONS

ROBIN JONES GUNN

When we lived in Reno, Rachel had a best friend named Kristin. We moved to Portland only a few days before Rachel's first day of second grade. Each night we talked about her new school and prayed together before she went to bed. The night before school started Rachel prayed that Jesus would give her a new best friend at this school and that her name would be Kristin. I felt compelled to alter her prayer but decided to let it go. *How do I tell my child she shouldn't be so specific with God?*

The next morning Rachel stood in front of the mirror while I combed her hair. She seemed lost in thought, and then suddenly she announced to me that Jesus was going to give her a new best friend. Her name would be Kristin, and she would have brown hair, just like the Kristin in Reno.

I quickly ran through all my mental notes on prayer. What would be the best way to explain to this child that prayer is not telling God what we have in mind for Him to do, but rather seeking His mind? I tried a few flimsy sentences. All fell flat. She seemed undaunted. I drove her to school still unable to find a way to protect her from her own prayer. I was afraid she would experience a spiritual crisis when she arrived at school and found no brunette Kristin in her class. What would that do to her innocent faith?

We entered the classroom, and Rachel found her name on her new desk. She lifted the top and began to examine the contents. I sat down at the desk next to hers and decided this would be a good time to explain how praying isn't like wishing. It's not magic. You can't ask God for something and expect it to materialize at your command. She needed to be willing to accept whatever new friends God brought to her.

I was about to plunge in, when out of the corner of my eye I noticed the name of the student who would occupy the desk next to Rachel. There, in bold letters, was printed Kristin.

I could barely speak. "Rachel," I finally managed in a whisper, "look! There *is* a Kristin in your class. And she's going to sit right next to you!"

"I know, Mom. She's the one I prayed for."

The bell rang, and I practically staggered to the back of the classroom as the students began to come in. Rachel sat up straight, folded her hands on her desk, and grinned confidently.

I glued my eyes to that door. Four boys entered. Then a girl with blonde hair who took a seat in the first row. Two more boys and then, there she was! She sauntered shyly to the "Kristin" desk, caught Rachel's welcoming grin, and returned the same.

I probably don't need to mention that she had brown hair—down to her waist.

Or, that everything I really needed to know about prayer I learned in second grade.

A SPECIAL FRIEND

KELSEY TYLER

Bob and Sue Nobles had been married nearly five years when they learned in 1979 that Sue was pregnant. Since they had been trying to have a baby for several years and were both in their late thirties, they were thrilled with the news.

"I hope it's a girl," Bob told Sue, a pretty woman with dark hair and green eyes. "And I hope she looks just like you."

Sue smiled and wondered how she would ever survive the nine-month wait until she could hold their baby in her arms.

"I can't believe it's finally happening," she said. "And you know, I really don't care if it's a girl or boy! I just hope our child is healthy."

Bob placed an arm casually across Sue's shoulders. "Don't worry, honey," he said. "Everything will be fine."

When Nicolette Jane Nobles—Coley—was born in March 1980, everything seemed perfect. Their tiny daughter was beautiful with a head full of dark curls and delicately etched features. But after several months Bob and Sue began to notice another difference between her and other children her age. She was silent. Whereas children her age whom they might see in the supermarket or at church would coo or say simple words, Coley rarely uttered any sound at all.

Finally the parents arranged an appointment with a specialist who was able to confirm their fears. Coley had been born deaf and would remain so for the rest of her life. On the drive home from the doctor's office, Coley sat in the back seat playing with a stuffed animal while Bob and Sue held hands and shared their grief over the news.

"I want so much for her to be like the other kids," Sue said, wiping the tears from her cheeks. "It just isn't fair. She's such a beautiful girl, and now she's going to be different from her peers for the rest of her life."

Bob stared straight ahead, keeping his eyes on the road. "I keep thinking that she'll never hear the sound of our voices."

Sue and Bob vowed that day always to be strong for Coley and to expect only the best from her in every situation. They would never allow her to use her deafness as an excuse for doing anything less than she was capable of. They agreed to learn sign language and to teach Coley as soon as possible. And they would also teach her to read lips so that she would have an easier time fitting in with other children in a school setting. They knew there would be times of disappointment and setbacks, but they promised to lean on each other and give Coley the best life possible despite her handicap.

As the years passed, the Nobles lived up to their promise. While she was a toddler, Coley learned to speak to her parents in sign language, and soon she was making progress in her ability to read lips.

Teaching Coley to make friends with hearing children proved to be the most difficult aspect of helping her learn to live with her deafness. As a toddler, Coley was introduced to lots of children her age but never seemed to fit in with them. Once while at the park, she tried to talk in sign language to a young girl who was obviously able to hear.

"Want to play with my dolly?" Coley signed quickly.

The child gave Coley a blank stare and looked at her hands. "Why are you moving your hands like that?" the girl asked out loud.

Coley looked at the girl curiously, unable to understand her lip movement, and then once again used sign language to ask the girl if she wanted to play. This time the child began to laugh at Coley, assuming that Coley was playing some kind of game.

But the girl's laughter confused Coley, and she began to cry, turning and running to where her mother sat painfully watching the exchange from a nearby park bench.

"It's all right," Sue signed to her daughter, taking her into her arms. "She wants to be your friend, honey, she just didn't understand you."

"She didn't like me," Coley signed back to her mother. Sue's heart went out to her daughter, whose tiny spirit seemed crushed by the encounter.

"No, Coley," Sue signed in return. "She liked you a lot. She just didn't understand you."

But Coley seemed frightened, and Sue thought she knew why. For the first time the little girl understood that she was different from other children, and the thought must have terrified her. After that she refused to make any attempt to communicate with other children. She would play near them and smile at them, but she always remained an outsider.

"What are we going to do, Bob?" a weary Sue complained one night. "I've tried to help her make friends with other children, but she's afraid to make an effort, afraid they won't like her."

"Give it time, honey," Bob said, sitting down at the table across from his wife. "She has a lot of adjusting to do, and she's come so far in such a few years. She'll have friends one day."

Susan was quiet for a moment. "Bob," she finally said softly. "Have you prayed about it, I mean about this friendship thing?"

Bob looked sad as he answered. "Not really. I mean, of course I've prayed for Coley. I've prayed for her since the day she was born. But I haven't really asked God to send her a special friend, if that's what you mean."

Sue nodded. "Well, let's do it. Let's pray together and then let's keep praying every day that God will love Coley enough to send her a special friend."

Bob reached across the table and took Sue's hands. Together they bowed their heads and prayed. Quietly, sincerely, they asked that Coley be watched over and cared for and that God would find it in His heart to give Coley a special friend.

After that, Bob and Sue prayed daily for Coley and the friend she might one day have. Later that year Coley turned five and began attending a school for children with special needs. Academically she excelled far beyond her parents' dreams, but she still struggled socially.

One day she came home with her head high and, as much as an adult would, asked her mother to sit with her on the couch and talk for a while.

"I'm deaf, right, Mommy?" she signed.

Sue paused a moment. They had dealt with Coley's deafness since the day she was diagnosed, but they had never discussed with her exactly what made her different from other children. "Yes, Cole," Sue moved her hands gently, her eyes searching those of her daughter's. "You were born without the ability to hear sound."

"And that makes me different, right, Mommy?" she asked.

Sue sighed, feeling the tears well up in her eyes. "Yes, honey. Most children can hear sounds. But there are many children who are born deaf, just like you."

"Even though I'm deaf, I'm still smart and I'm still pretty, and I'm still special. Isn't that right, Mommy?" Coley's eyes shone as she asked the question, and Sue struggled to keep from crying. "And God still loves me, right?"

"Of course, Coley, God loves you very much. You are very special and beautiful and very wonderful and being deaf will never change that."

Coley thought for a moment. Then her hands began to move once again. "It's time for me to have a friend, Mommy. . . . But I want a friend who's deaf like me. Is that okay?"

Sue pulled her daughter close and wrapped her arms around her, stroking her silky dark curls. "I've been asking God to send you a special friend, Coley. Maybe that's what He has in mind. A special friend who is deaf like you. We'll just have to wait and see."

The year ran its course, and although Coley made more of an attempt with the other children than she had in the past, none of her classmates were deaf, and she finished her first year of school without a close friend.

A few months before her sixth birthday, Coley stumbled upon a picture of a white Persian kitten in one of her storybooks. She was immediately and completely enamored with the kitten and ran to show her mother the picture.

"Mommy, can I please have a kitten like that for my birthday? Please?" Coley was so animated that Sue had to calm her down before her daughter would show her the picture in the book.

"That's a Persian kitten, Coley," Sue said as she looked at the picture. "You want a kitten like that?"

"Yes, yes, yes," Coley signed quickly. "Please, Mommy," she pleaded.

Later that night Sue and Bob discussed the idea of getting a kitten for Coley's birthday.

"She's always loved her stuffed animals," Sue said as she presented the idea. "Maybe that's just what she needs right now. A pet of her own."

"But a white Persian kitten?" Bob asked. "They cost hundreds of dollars, Sue. You know that we can't afford that."

Bob was a teacher and Sue worked part-time at Coley's school. With the cost of their daughter's special education, they were barely able to scrape enough money together to meet their monthly needs.

"I know," Sue said. "But maybe we could save for the next few weeks and watch the advertisements in the newspaper. Maybe there'll be one for sale that we can afford."

Bob thought a moment and sighed. "All right, let's try it. But don't say anything to Coley about it. I'd hate to get her hopes up."

For the next seven weeks Sue scanned the newspapers for white Persian kittens and found none for sale. Finally, a few days before Coley's birthday, she and Bob decided they had barely saved enough money to purchase a kitten if only they could find one.

On the morning of Coley's birthday, while the little girl was still sleeping, Sue opened the newspaper and pored over the classified advertisements. Suddenly she gasped out loud.

"Bob! They're here. The kittens. Persian kittens, white, two hundred dollars. Can you believe it! That's where we're going to get Coley's kitten."

When the child woke up, they gave her a card and her favorite pancake breakfast and told her that they were going to take her that afternoon to buy a white Persian kitten. Coley's mouth flew open and her eyes grew wide.

"Oh, thank you, thank you," she signed repeatedly. "When do we get him?"

Sue walked over to the phone as she signed, "Let's call them right now."

While Coley waited impatiently watching her mother, Sue dialed the number that had been listed in the advertisement.

"Yes," she said when someone answered the phone. "I'm calling about the white Persian kittens."

On the other line Maria Amado smiled. "Oh, yes," she said. "We have a few left and they're both the same, white kittens with gray markings."

"Oh." Sue's face fell in disappointment, and Coley watched closely, trying to read her mother's lips. "We were looking for one that is completely white. It's for my daughter's birthday."

"I see," Maria said. "Well, there is one kitten that's completely white. I'll sell her to you for fifty dollars instead of the two hundred dollars if you're interested."

"I don't understand," Sue said, her face puzzled.

"Well," Maria paused, "the kitten is deaf. I'm not sure if I'll be able to sell her."

Sue began to shake, and for a moment she was unable to speak. Aware that something strange was happening, Coley began signing frantically. "What, Mommy? What is it?"

"Are you still there?" Maria asked, breaking the silence.

"Yes! Um, just a minute," Sue said. She turned toward her daughter and set the receiver down on the counter. Stooping to Coley's level, she quickly began moving her hands. "The kitten is a girl kitten, and it's deaf, Coley. A deaf white Persian kitten."

Coley's face lit up as Sue had never seen it do before. "That's my kitten, Mommy!" she said. "Let's go get her."

Within an hour, Sue, Bob, and Coley arrived at Maria's house. Maria explained how the other kittens would run and hide when she ran the vacuum, but the white kitten seemed unaffected by the noise. Bob and Sue exchanged a knowing glance, remembering the days when they were trying to figure out what was wrong with Coley.

"Eventually I had the kitten checked by a veterinarian, and she told us the poor little thing was deaf," Maria told them.

Sue held the kitten and handed him to Coley. Her hands began to move. "See, Coley. She's perfect and beautiful and special, just like the other kittens. The only difference is she can't hear."

Coley smiled, snuggling her face up close to the kitten's. Then she looked at her mother and with her free hand said, "Let's take her home, Mommy."

Over the next few weeks there was no separating Coley and her tiny deaf kitten. Every afternoon she would set the kitten in front of her on the bed and use sign language to talk to her. One day Sue watched, trying to understand what Coley was telling the kitten.

"It's okay, Kitty," Coley said, her little hands moving slowly so her kitten could understand. "You don't have to be afraid or lonely anymore because now there's two deaf people in our family. We'll be best friends forever."

Sue walked into the room slowly and sat down next to Coley.

"You love her don't you, Cole?" she signed to her daughter.

"Yes, Mommy. She and I are both special because we're both deaf." Coley looked at her kitten, whose soft white face was tilted curiously as she watched Coley's fingers move. Coley looked back at her mother. "She doesn't understand sign language yet, but when she gets older she will. And then it will be easier for her to talk with me."

Coley reached for the kitten and held her close. "Thank you for praying, Mommy. God heard your prayers," she signed. "He gave me a friend who was born deaf just like me."

"Yes, Cole," Sue smiled. "I was just thinking that. God definitely heard our prayers."

THE IMPOSSIBLE SEARCH

DANIEL CAREY

When I discovered I had lost my wedding ring I was upset. It wasn't just a piece of jewelry; it was the symbol of a vital turning point in my life.

That November evening I searched everywhere, rummaging through clothes pockets, ransacking drawers, peering under beds. I nearly drove my wife, Mary, and our two daughters crazy asking them if they had seen it.

Mary understood my desperation; the ring meant a lot to her too. She had put it on my finger at a time when life had begun anew for both of us. That was in 1978, ten years *after* we had married.

We first met in the late sixties in San Francisco. I was living in the Haight-Ashbury district, a counterculture guy managing a rock 'n' roll band. One day I went to make a deposit at the bank; Mary was a teller there. When we decided to get married, my mother came from Boston for the wedding, and was shocked to learn we didn't plan on exchanging wedding bands. "Who needs rings?" I asked.

"You must have rings!" my mom insisted. So, early on the morning of our wedding day, I bought two metal bands for three dollars each.

Marriage didn't make me settle down. Even when our lovely little girl Marta was born, I kept drinking and smoking and carousing up a storm. By then I was working in construction, and as I hauled, lifted and sawed, my three-dollar wedding band kept getting bent and worn, pretty much like my marriage. God was trying to tell me something, I believe, when one day my wedding ring broke into three pieces.

But I wasn't listening to God or anyone else. Not until I staggered into the house one night to find it cold, dark and empty did reality hit me. Mary had taken Marta and moved out, gone to Sparks, Nevada, where her parents lived.

I lurched into the bathroom and stood gazing at my blotched face in the mirror. I didn't like what I saw. For the first time I realized I had a choice—continue as I was, or pray to God for the strength to change.

With God's help I was able to stop drinking and smoking. As my thinking became clearer, I realized what a treasure I had lost.

By the time 1978 approached, I was on the phone to Mary. She could tell I had changed, and soon we were laughing together like old times. "Dan," she said, "let's get back together." In no time flat I packed my car, called the movers and drove to Sparks, where I got a job.

Now it was time for *real* wedding rings. We had heard about an unusual jewelry store in Nevada City, California, where one of the owners panned for gold nuggets and his partner fashioned them into rings. Mary and I drove there and bought beautiful gold rings inlaid with nuggets. Solid and enduring, they were symbols of our new life together. When we placed those bands on each other's fingers, it was one of the happiest days of my life.

Eventually we moved to New England, where our second daughter, Allison, was born. We worked hard and were successful. By 1986 we had settled in a new home in Worthington, Massachusetts, and were counting our blessings. And foremost among them was our restored marriage.

So when I discovered my gold nugget wedding ring was missing, I couldn't believe I had been so careless. For a week I searched everywhere, crawling around the woodpile, emptying vacuum-cleaner bags, taking the seats out of the car and probing between the cushions. Nothing. Meanwhile, I did a lot of praying, asking God to help.

"This is important to me," I told Him. Then one day a week after the ring disappeared, I was washing my hands in the kitchen sink when our cat jumped up on the counter. "Hey, Patches," I said, "you're not supposed to do that."

Suddenly a picture flashed in my mind: I remembered starting to do the dishes, removing the ring and placing it on the very spot where the cat had just landed. I looked down to see our wastebasket directly below. And I *knew*. The cat had knocked the ring into the garbage.

When I yelled to Mary, her face turned pale. "You've already taken our garbage to the town Dumpster!"

"I know, I know!" I exclaimed. When I got to where the Dumpster had been, it was gone. Breathless, I raced to the rubbish-removal company. "I think my wedding ring might be in the garbage," I sputtered.

The girl in the office stared in disbelief. "Tons of refuse from the last Dumpster pickup have been compacted and put on a truck," she said.

"Where does the truck take it?"

"To a big landfill in Granby." That was some twenty miles away. "It's scheduled to go Monday."

Any rational person would have turned around and gone home. But I couldn't give up. *God, this is important to me.* "Can't I go to the dump?" I begged. "I've *got* to find my ring."

When it was clear I wasn't going away, the girl reached for the phone. "Hello, landfill office? Could our driver unload tomorrow in an area where it's relatively flat and clean? We've got a guy here who wants to try to find something he's lost." From the sound of the voices on the other end I knew the landfill people couldn't believe it either. "I know. I told him there's *tons* of garbage on that truck," she said. "But he wants to try anyway." When she hung up, she was smiling. "Yes, they'll do it."

So on a gray, sleeting Monday afternoon in November, I drove behind the truck, my windshield wipers seeming to smack me with every swipe: *What you're doing is hope . . . less. Hope . . . less. Hope . . . less.*

The truck's brakes wheezed as it pulled into a gigantic landfill, where mountains of rubbish sprawled to the horizon. In the distance a bulldozer groaned under a canopy of wheeling, squawking seagulls.

It was around 2:30 P.M. as driver Greg Hurlburt ejected the garbage from the truck. As the compressed refuse—mostly plastic garbage bags—cascaded onto the ground, there was a hiss as much of it puffed up again. Now there was a wall of garbage some six feet high and maybe seventy feet long. To me it looked like the Great Wall of China. All of a sudden I felt like an idiot. It seemed impossible to find a Volkswagon in all that stuff, much less an object about the size of a quarter.

Greg jumped down from his cab with a grin. "Okay, where do we start?" he asked.

"*We?*" I responded. "You're going to help me dig in all this?"

"Sure," he said. "I think your Dumpster load should be"—he strode along and pointed—"somewhere around here."

Even if Greg were right, "somewhere around here" involved hundreds of bags packed to capacity. "You drink or smoke?" he asked. I shook my head no—emphatically—to that one. "You can spot liquor bottles and cigarette cartons in a lot of the bags," Greg pointed out. "So we know your ring's not in those."

We waded into the sea of refuse. By then freezing rain was running down our necks. "We're never going to find that ring!" I shouted. But Greg was having none of it.

"Don't say 'never,'" he yelled back. "You're *gonna* find it!"

God, this is important to me. I pulled loose a bag, and a circle of blue-gray caught my eye. Colonial blue-gray. Just like the shutters we had recently painted on our house! I let out a yelp and ripped open the bag. Yes, it was a paint-can lid! But no sign of the ring.

Greg picked up another bag, only to have its bottom give out, the contents tumbling into the muck. We groped through it all. "Here, try this one." Greg passed a bag to me, I dropped it and gave a yank . . . inside was a crushed egg carton. And nestled in an indentation gleamed—my gold-nugget wedding ring!

Greg and I clapped each other on the back and howled with glee.

When I got back home with the ring, Mary was astounded. She and I celebrated by going out to dinner. At the table Mary slipped the ring back onto my finger, and softly repeated the words we had said so many years ago: "With this ring, I thee wed."

"You know, Honey," I said, "everybody thought I was nuts for going to all that trouble."

"I didn't," she said, smiling.

NOTHING AT ALL TOO SMALL

JOAN WESTER ANDERSON

On a cold Sunday afternoon a few years ago, David Miller, age thirteen, and his ten-year-old brother, Nicholas, decided to go sledding on a hill just a short distance from their home in South Sioux City, Nebraska. The hill was covered with six inches of new snow, and trails had been cut into it by earlier sledders, making it especially fun. The boys and their friends were having a wonderful time, and then disaster struck. Whizzing downhill, David's sled hit a bump. "Oh, no!" he shouted as he tried to brake. "My glasses just flew off!"

"Uh-oh." Nicholas didn't wear glasses, but he knew how important they were. He and David would have to find them right away before they were trampled by the other kids or buried until spring!

The boys searched for almost an hour, going up and down the hill on each side of the many sled trails, even looking on the edges near the highway and in the tall broom grass that poked above the drifts. They found nothing. Finally, as dusk approached, they trudged home and reported the loss to their father, Dave.

Dave is somewhat of an optimist. A deacon in the South Sioux Assembly of God church, he's a husband and father of four, and considers himself a fortunate man. Although the sun was already down, he thought he and the boys should look again. Surely the glasses would turn up.

The three headed back to the hill. But by now, young David no longer remembered which trail he had been sledding on, or whether his glasses had flown off nearer the top or the bottom of the hill. "I began to realize that there had been hordes of kids playing here all day, and probably someone had accidentally crushed them underfoot already," Dave said. As darkness fell, they gave up. But Dave decided to try again the next morning. He would use his metal detector, one of his favorite hobby items, although, he says, "It doesn't get much of a workout in the snow."

But the next morning the Miller family awakened to the worst of all scenarios. Two inches of new snow had fallen during the night. "I like a challenge," Dave says, "but this was certainly like looking for the proverbial needle in the haystack." Still, he took a rake and his metal detector and went back to the hill. Before starting his painstaking task, he remembered to check the batteries in the metal detector. They were dead. How could that be? He had just replaced them this morning.

Sighing, Dave laid the useless machine down and began to rake. It was his only option. Inch by painstaking inch, he worked his way up the first sled trail. His toes froze. People driving by gave him strange looks. He started on the second trail, but he wasn't getting anywhere.

This was stupid. It was impossible. He would have to give up. Suddenly Dave heard a little voice inside him. "Did you ever think to *pray?*" the voice chided him gently. "Did you ever consider asking God to find the glasses?" Dave felt humbled and embarrassed all at the same time. He, a deacon at his church, had been so head-strong, so *in charge*, that he hadn't even thought to begin at the beginning! Without a thought for the drivers who would see him as they passed, Dave knelt down in the snow, folded his hands, and closed his eyes.

"God, I'm sorry that I forgot about You," he whispered. "I try never to do that, not for a minute. Please forgive me now. And please find the glasses." He stayed silent a moment longer, then opened his eyes.

In front of him lay David's glasses. Despite last night's snowfall, they were in plain view and in perfect condition, resting on a clump of broom grass directly in his path. They looked, Dave realized, as if they had been waiting to be found.

"I have always believed in miracles, but so often they seem to happen to some-one else," Dave says. And maybe that's because *we* so often forget to ask. "The glasses reminded me that He wants to be involved in every part of our lives. No problem is too small for God."

Chapter 2   Grace for Special Needs

Stories of how God provides are thrilling. From God's provision of manna and quail to the multiplication of the loaves and fish, we know that God supplies the needs of His children. These may be our basic physical needs, such as hunger, shelter, clothing and transportation, or our more essential needs, like courage or faith or hope; again and again we witness God's faithfulness as He provides for us.

Ironically, it is our utter poverty that makes the touch of God's grace so sweet when we receive it. Our anxiety and fear, so acute when we struggle to figure out how we will manage, is replaced with peace and a profound sense of well-being. And in time, we learn that God does care for us, not simply in the abstract, but in the most personal and practical ways. He loves us enough to see that our bills are paid and our children are fed. And we learn that we do not need to panic or despair or worry.

Jesus understood God's care intimately and described it in his Sermon on the Mount: *". . . your Father knows what you need before you ask him. . . . Therefore I tell you, do not worry about your life, what you will eat or drink; or about your body, what you will wear. Is not life more important than food, and the body more important than clothes? Look at the birds of the air; they do not sow or reap or store away in barns, and yet your heavenly Father feeds them. Are you not much more valuable than they? Who of you by worrying can add a single hour to his life?*

"And why do you worry about clothes? See how the lilies of the field grow. They do not labor or spin. Yet I tell you that not even Solomon in all his splendor was dressed like one of these. If that is how God clothes the grass of the field, which is here today and tomorrow is thrown into the fire, will he not much more clothe you, O you of little faith? So do not worry, saying, 'What shall we eat?' or 'What shall we drink?' or 'What shall we wear?' For the pagans run after all these things, and your heavenly Father knows that you need them. But seek first his kingdom and his righteousness, and all these things will be given to you as well. Therefore do not worry about tomorrow, for tomorrow will worry about itself. Each day has enough trouble of its own" (Matthew 6:28–34, NIV).

> *O Tender Father, You gave me more, much more than I ever thought to ask for. I realize that our human desires can never really match what you long to give us. Thanks, and again thanks, O Father, for having granted my petitions, and that which I never realized I needed or petitioned. Amen.*
>
> —St. Catherine of Siena (1347–1380)

A PERFECT MISTAKE

CHERYL WALTERMAN STEWART

Grandpa Nybakken loved life—especially when he could play a trick on somebody. At those times, his large Norwegian frame shook with laughter while he feigned innocent surprise, exclaiming, "Oh, forevermore!" But on a cold Saturday in downtown Chicago, Grandpa felt that God played a trick on him, and Grandpa wasn't laughing.

Mother's father worked as a carpenter. On this particular day, he was building some crates for the clothes his church was sending to an orphanage in China. On his way home, he reached into his shirt pocket to find his glasses, but they were gone. He remembered putting them there that morning, so he drove back to the church. His search seemed fruitless.

When he mentally replayed his earlier actions, he realized what had happened. The glasses had slipped out of his pocket unnoticed and fallen into one of the crates, which he had nailed shut. His brand new glasses were heading for China!

Times were hard, and Grandpa had six children. He had spent twenty dollars for those glasses that very morning. "It's not fair," he told God as he drove home in frustration. "I've been very faithful in giving of my time and money to your work, and now this."

Several months later, the director of the orphanage was on furlough in the United States, so he came to speak one Sunday night at my grandfather's small church in Chicago. Grandpa and his family sat in their customary seats among the sparse congregation.

The missionary began by thanking the people for their faithfulness in supporting the orphanage.

"But most of all," he said, "I must thank you for the glasses you sent last year. You see, the Communists had just swept through the orphanage, destroying everything, including my glasses. I was desperate.

"Even if I had the money, there was simply no way of replacing those glasses. Along with not being able to see well, I experienced headaches every day, so my co-workers and I were much in prayer about this. Then your crates arrived. When my staff removed the covers, they found a pair of glasses lying on top."

The missionary paused long enough to let the words sink in. Then, still gripped with the wonder of it all, he continued, "Folks, when I tried on those glasses, it was as though they had been custom-made just for me! I want to thank you for being a part of that."

The people listened, happy for the miraculous glasses. But the missionary surely must have confused their church with another, they thought. There were no glasses on their list of items to be sent overseas.

But sitting quietly in the back, with tears streaming down his face, an ordinary carpenter realized the Master Carpenter had used him in an extraordinary way.

RAISINS AND ALMONDS

AFTON CORNELL HARVEY

A month and a half before I turned fourteen—many, many years ago—my mother gave birth to Norman. He came barely a year after my brother Dean. Norman wasn't supposed to arrive until a month *after* my birthday.

"Nonie," as Daddy dubbed brother Norman, weighed a sickly five pounds. To make matters worse, Mother was unable to breast-feed him and Nonie could not tolerate formula. No matter what variety we tried, poor little Nonie spat it up. He grew pale and weak, with deep dark circles under his eyes. One night Mother gathered us six children to pray and ask the Lord that some milk be found that would agree with Nonie.

As the oldest I took responsibility for little Dean in order to give Mother more time with the new baby. That summer I often pushed Dean around our Salt Lake City neighborhood in a big wicker baby buggy. One day as I was passing a duplex on University Avenue, a block from home, a young woman in her mid twenties stepped down from her porch. She was short with curly brown hair. Her eye harbored a hint of anxiety, I thought. Standing in the open doorway behind her were a little boy and girl.

The woman made small talk for a few minutes, then asked: "Could you and your baby brother come inside to visit?"

Bored with my duties and glad for the company, I accepted. On a blanket in the living room lay the prettiest baby girl I had ever seen. Her mother grabbed her and kissed her. "I call her Dimples," she said. The two older children, Danny and Annie, quickly went off to play.

The woman took Dean and put him on the floor with some toys, then settled on the couch and began to talk. She seemed starved for company. I was pretty desperate for someone to talk with too, having spent most of the summer minding Dean.

Her name was Annette. Her husband, who worked for a furniture-store chain, had recently been transferred to Salt Lake City from the East. "Work keeps him so busy I hardly ever see him," she said with a sigh. "He travels a lot." Looking at her baby she added, "And I just don't have the chance to get out and meet people."

"Would you like something to drink?" she asked suddenly, as if she were a little shocked at her own lack of hospitality. But I knew she was so glad for someone to talk to that she had forgotten to offer. I told her I would take a root beer, and got more comfortable on the couch. Annette said she was from a New York City neighborhood called Washington Heights. "That's where all my friends and relatives live," She said wistfully. "I sure miss them, especially my sisters and Mama. I miss her good Jewish cooking."

I tried not to look surprised. I had never met a Jewish person before.

"What's Jewish cooking?" I asked.

"You've never had it?" Annette laughed, smoothing my hair. Then she described tasty noodle pudding, kreplachs and matzo ball soup. "No one cooks like my mother," she said, and I thought I detected a tremor in her voice.

"You'll come back and visit again?" Annette asked after I told her it was time to go.

"You bet!" I replied, waving goodbye to my new friends as I pushed Dean's buggy down the street.

I became a regular visitor. Dean played with Dimples while Annette and I swapped stories about our childhoods. Occasionally I watched her three children so she could go shopping. Although we always had fun, there was a sadness about Annette, as if something troubled her that I was too young to understand. I didn't feel right asking her about it, though. One day as I watched Annette nursing Dimples, I couldn't help exclaiming, "Oh, I wish my mother could feed Nonie like that!"

Annette looked at me, puzzled.

"Our new baby at home," I explained. "He was premature. The doctor can't find the right formula for him. Mother's afraid we'll lose him."

"How old is . . . ?"

"Nonie. He's seven weeks."

Annette wiped milk from her baby's mouth and turned to me. "Let's all go over to your house right now, Afton. I have an idea."

Mother was surprised to see us. I introduced Annette, who, without preamble, announced, "I've come to nurse your baby."

Mother and I stared at each other, too surprised to speak. I could see how worry and exhaustion had etched lines deep into her face. She had all but given up hope on the doctor's finding the right formula, and had put her faith in God. Was Annette, who wasn't even our religion, God's answer?

While I pondered the situation, Mother scooped up Nonie and handed him to Annette, who sat down and unbuttoned her blouse. As we watched, Nonie sucked long and hungrily. After a few minutes, when the only sounds came from my baby brother's busy mouth, Annette began to croon a lullaby, *Rozinkes un Mandlen.* "In Yiddish it means 'Raisins and Almonds,'" she explained. "It's a song a mother sings to her child, hoping for a better future."

When Nonie was satisfied, Mother picked him up. And at his little burp, tears tumbled down her cheeks. "I don't know how to thank you," she said.

"Please," Annette said, "you don't need to thank me."

From then on that summer, twice a day, Annette walked over with her children to nurse Nonie. His once listless eyes became bright and merry and his face filled out. What surprised me more, though, was the change in Annette. She seemed to draw a kind of nourishment from Nonie. The worry in her eyes faded a little each day.

"You are an answer to our prayers," I heard Mother tell Annette one afternoon.

"Not much as you are to mine," Annette replied. "More than you know."

Each week my brother grew stronger. Soon he was eating solid foods too. Then one crisp October afternoon Annette told us she was returning to New York.

Mother cried, threw her arms around Annette and told her how much she loved her for saving Nonie's life. Annette touched a finger to Mother's lips and said, "*Sshhh. What you must know is that Nonie, Afton and you have saved *my* life. The day I first met Afton I felt such loneliness and despair that I had decided I just couldn't endure life any longer."

She looked at the floor. "God forgive me for what I thought about doing." Then, wiping her eyes, she looked up. "He must have known what was in my mind because he sent Afton."

Over the next couple of days, while I helped Annette pack, she explained that she was returning to her family without her husband. She and her children would begin new lives. Without needing it explained in detail, I knew the sadness Annette felt had been caused by her husband.

Even then I understood adults could cause one another incredible pain. That long-ago summer I learned how God could ease our pain. We had asked him for milk for Nonie. God responded by making our prayer the answer to a neighbor's desperate need. We never saw or talked to Annette after she returned east. All I know is the sadness seemed to drain out of her as she nursed my baby brother and sang a lullaby about raisins and almonds and hope for a better future—and the nourishment of God's love in our lives.

DIVINE CALCULATION

Lois Spoon

Time was running out. I needed $153.27 by 2:00 P.M. and it was already 1:30 P.M. I was confident that God would meet my need for this amount when the time came, but this was cutting it awfully close.

I sat in my car outside a restaurant where I had just eaten lunch with several ladies from my church. When it came time to pay for the meal, I picked up the tab of a guest missionary from Romania, using my last twenty dollars.

God will provide my need, I said confidently to myself. But my certainty began to waver as the breeze blew through my car windows. No one else knew about my dilemma.

What should I do? Keys still clutched in my hand, I laid my head back against the headrest and thought of the verse in Matthew 17:27 that tells how Jesus' disciples needed money to pay their taxes. He told them to go out on the lake and the first fish they caught would have a coin in its mouth that would cover the amount they needed.

"Dear Lord," I prayed. "I need a fish soon. Please show me where to find the lake."

There was no doubt in my mind that God had provided the opportunity I'd been given to fly to Indianapolis, Indiana, with a physical therapist friend. We were to attend a workshop on "lymphodema," open only to doctors and physical therapists. I was neither.

But I suffered from this condition that caused tremendous swelling in my arm, a result of surgery for cancer. Because my physical therapist knew of the great interest I had in the subject, she arranged for me to attend with her. On top of that, every expense would be paid, except my plane fare of $153.27.

I eagerly accepted her invitation and started asking God to help provide the money for me to go. I knew from the start it would take a miracle because our budget was stretched as tight as it could go toward medical bills incurred fighting the cancer. But it wasn't hard for me to believe in miracles—I was living proof!

Since God had chosen to heal me of cancer, I reasoned, but this condition remained, there must be a reason. Maybe He wanted to use me to help find a cure for this problem, which affects millions of people. Before me was a rare opportunity to research and learn more about the condition from a medical point of view.

I was to meet my friend in a half hour at the travel agency to pay for and pick up my plane ticket.

I glanced in my rear-view mirror and saw a small black sports car back out, then pull back into its parking space. As I watched, it backed out again and I recognized the driver as Beverly Easton, a lady from my luncheon group.

I wondered if she was having car trouble when she slowly drove out of the parking lot, circled the restaurant, and pulled back in again. This time she stopped in the middle of the lot, got out, and walked toward my car. Maybe she thinks I'm having car trouble. Beverly stuck her head through my open passenger window.

"I know you don't know me very well and I hope you don't think I'm crazy," she said. "I'm so embarrassed. Please don't be offended by this."

My curiosity was stirred. "What's the matter, Beverly?"

"Well," she hesitated. "Several months ago God told me to put change in an envelope for you. I've just carried it around and been adding to it every day till I got the nerve to give it to you. I hope this isn't insulting."

Her face flamed red as she tossed a bulging envelope onto the car seat.

"I just have to obey God," she mumbled, darting to her car before I could respond.

Makeup smudges and ink smears covered the once white envelope. On the front, my name was scribbled in big letters and there was a card inside explaining that she wasn't sure why, but God had told her to give me this money. It was dated several months earlier. With tears in my eyes, I carefully emptied the contents out on the seat and started counting. There were bills of all denominations and lots of change.

The Bible says in Hebrews 13:8 that God is the same yesterday, today and forever. If He provided His followers in Bible days with what they needed, He can and will do the same for His followers today. What an awesome God He is.

This time it wasn't a lake He used, but a lady named Beverly. And it wasn't a fish, but an envelope. One that contained exactly $153.27.

CONSTRUCTION AHEAD

JOAN WESTER ANDERSON

My nephew Tom Anderson received a heavenly go-ahead. Tom is a cabinet-maker, and after working for others for several years, he decided to go solo. He wanted to do the kind of fine woodcrafting that satisfied him right down to his soul.

But searching for customers, meeting his overhead and doing the work itself took more time than Tom had figured. He also grappled with tax forms, bookkeeping and a slew of new responsibilities he neither wanted nor enjoyed. His dream was rapidly turning into an exhausting treadmill.

One morning as he sped along to an appointment, Tom found himself rethinking his plans. Had he made the right decision? He had prayed about it beforehand and felt sure that God approved, but now he was having second thoughts. "God, I'm overwhelmed," he sighed. "Should I go back to a safe nine-to-five job without all this worry? Please tell me what You want me to do."

Just then Tom passed a parked police car and realized with a sinking heart that he was going at least twenty-five miles over the speed limit. In his rearview mirror, he saw the car move out and flash its lights. Great. Tom pulled over and slumped dejectedly in the seat. Not only would he be even later to his appointment, he sure had his answer now. How much more negative a signal could God send?

"License and registration, please." The officer approached Tom's truck, ticket book in hand.

"Yes, sir." Tom didn't even put up a defense. He was so disappointed at the thought of giving up his goals that he barely glanced at the officer until a moment or two had passed. Then he realized the officer was looking at his tools, stacked in the front seat because his new truck didn't yet have a cover.

The policeman gestured at them. "What do you do for a living?" he asked.

"I'm a cabinetmaker." Tom's curiosity mounted. *What did this have to do with a traffic stop?*

The officer handed Tom his license—without a ticket. "Go slower next time," he said. "And wear your seat belt." Tom could hardly believe it. But the officer wasn't finished. He leaned against Tom's truck. "I moonlight as a general contractor," he said. "And I've got sixteen custom kitchens and fifteen bathrooms that all need cabinets right now. Think you'd be interested?"

"It was a real answer, just what I had asked for," Tom says today as he runs his successful business. "God was saying 'Keep going—but slow down.' I know He'll always give me the directions I need."

MY ONLY PRAYER

LEE MAYNARD

We are hunkered down at the base of a rock overhang, the summit far above us, watching the rain fall softly. We are tired from climbing and running from the rain.

My eleven-year-old grandson, Tristan, is with me. He knows about Martian landings and cyberspace, and just when you think that's all he is—an interesting child of a technological age—he names the Greek gods and tells how the citizens prayed to them.

"Maybe we should pray for a way out of here," I say, watching the rain grow heavier.

"Does prayer really work?" he asks. "Would it really get us out of here?"

I think carefully about what to say next . . . for I am not a prayerful man.

I have had my share of hurts and pains in the wilderness. The stings of scorpions. The snapping of bones. Dehydration so severe my eyes stung. But I never prayed over any of that. I always thought that if I had put myself into those places, it was up to me to get out. God probably wasn't interested.

Prayer, I have always thought, was the thing you saved for last. But every time I got to the last, there was no time for praying. And when it was over, all I could do was wonder that I was still alive.

And so I never prayed. Except once.

It was 1978. In the early hours, when the tops of trees were still lost in darkness, I parked my truck and stepped into New Mexico's Gila Wilderness. My plan was to hike twenty miles in, then join up with a group of nine Outward Bound School students and their instructors, a "patrol." I was the school director, and I was worried about this patrol: three New England preppies, a college freshman, three high school graduates from Dallas and two South Chicago street kids who had been sentenced to Outward Bound in lieu of jail.

I looked forward to hiking in the Gila. Even after half a lifetime spent outdoors, I couldn't seem to see it enough. But it was midsummer, and the sun's heat poured down relentlessly. At midday I stopped, drank some water, and for the first time noticed the heat in my boots.

The boots were not new. I had worn them some weeks and thought they were ready for the Gila. I was wrong.

I tried everything for relief: stopped and aired my feet, put on extra socks, quickened my pace, slowed my pace, tightened my laces, applied moleskin. Nothing worked.

I reached camp in the middle of the evening meal, took off my boots and socks, and padded around on the soft forest floor. I inspected my feet and counted eleven blisters, near blisters and hot spots. Still, I told no one about my problem.

We sat and talked for hours. After two weeks in the wilderness, only one student, a New Englander, seemed disenchanted with the course. He had tried to quit but had been talked out of it by the staff.

In the morning, the New Englander was gone. He had left hours before, thrashing back down the trail I'd come in on. We couldn't just let him go into the unforgiving wilderness. Since I was the extra man, I put on the devil boots and went after him.

I soon realized I wasn't just limping anymore—I was walking as though barefoot on hot glass. As I shuffled and stumbled, I tried to keep my mind above my ankles. Again, nothing worked.

A new sound sucked its way into my consciousness, and I realized it was coming from my boots. I sat on a fallen tree, held my feet out in front of me, and looked at the crimson oozing from the eyelets. If I took the boots off, I would never get them on again.

Eventually the trail came out of the brush and straight into the Gila River, flowing down from the high country through shaded canyons. By the time it got to me, this narrow, shallow river was still icy, and I couldn't wait to feel it against my baking feet. But when the water poured into my boots, the burning sensation was replaced with a thousand stabs that seemed to puncture every blister.

My scream cut through the canyon, and I went face forward into the water. Then I got up and staggered across the river.

Since there was no rational solution to my problem, my mind began to create irrational ones. The answer, obviously, was a horse. If I just had a horse, my feet would no longer be a problem, and I could catch the New Englander.

Like King Richard III, I began to implore, "Give me another horse! Have mercy!" *What was the next word?* Oh, yes. "Jesu."

I knew I had only another hundred paces or so in me, and then I would stop, sit and wait. I'd probably see no one for days.

The sun was low against my back, and my shadow reached far down the stony trail. I would never get to the end of my shadow. And then I stopped.

The right shoulder of my shadow moved, a bulging darkness down on the trail. A huge mass, motionless now, blocked most of the low sun, an elongated head bobbing up in attention to my presence.

It was a horse. A ghost born of pain.

God, I thought, the mind is an amazing thing. It was a beautiful ghost, but I would have to make it go away. So I confronted it directly, dragging myself right up to the horse and grabbing its halter.

It was a real horse.

The animal had a halter and a lead rope but no saddle. Something was going on here that I didn't understand, but I was not going to question it. I gathered up the lead rope and struggled onto the horse's back. "A horse, a horse," I mumbled as it calmly carried me down the trail and into the falling darkness. "Jesu."

The horse walked through the night and did not stop until we got to the trail head, where I found the New Englander sitting on the bumper of my truck. I took off the hated boots, bandaged my feet, and hobbled the horse in a patch of grass. The New Englander and I slept nearby.

At first light two wranglers showed up looking for the horse. They said it had never wandered off before and didn't know why it did this time. They said the horse's name was King.

The rain turns to sleet, and I think maybe Tristan and I will have to sleep out the storm on a mountain where there are no horses. He leans against me, and he is smiling.

"Did you really pray?" he asks. "For a horse?"

"Well . . . I was a little out of it. Mumbling. I'm not sure anything I said would qualify as a prayer."

"I think you did pray," he says. "And you got what you prayed for, and it scared you." As usual, he's gotten to the heart of the matter.

The sleet disappears, and a thick mist suffuses the mountain. But behind the mist is a bright light, glowing first silver and then gold.

"I did, didn't I?" I admit. "I *did* pray."

We leave the overhang and start down the mountain, the air thick with the nectar of after-storm. It is one of the best days of my life.

Prayer still mystifies me. Maybe I shouldn't save it for last.

A PLACE PREPARED BY GOD

CATHERINE E. VERLENDEN

The green ceramic tiles of the bathroom floor cooled my baked-out skin. I sat back against the wall, my legs drawn up, clutching my Bible, folding into myself. And I wondered where this fear had come from, consuming enough to send me into the bathroom of a strange motel, hiding my torment from my sleeping sons in the next room.

Until then, I'd been doing pretty well. We'd made it through a sad divorce, and somehow God had given me the strength to move my young sons across the country to a new house, a new job, a new life. I'd felt capable and even excited.

But now, in the middle of the night, in the middle of nowhere, I saw myself for what I truly was: alone. And in danger.

The danger was not amorphous. It has a name: the Mojave Desert. And it was just outside the door.

So far we'd driven three days across the South, through sweltering July heat. My little car and I both had miles and experience under our fan belts, but we were still chugging along. Yet the trip, which had started so hopefully, had now turned sour. Perhaps it was the monotony of days of endless driving. During this last day, particularly, all the fears that had dogged me during the past difficult months found long stretches of thinking time to spend with me in the car.

As we neared the Mojave Desert, our final hurdle to our arrival in California, I realized the danger we faced and how vulnerable I was.

I'd heard every horror story—radiators that boil dry, blow-outs, relentless sun that crisps fragile flesh, the sheer isolation of the long asphalt strip that winds its way through the rocky desolation. Hours with no bathroom, no water . . . nothing. No help.

That frightened me the most. If we got into trouble, who would help us? How could I protect my children if the worst happened? They were dependent on *me,* and for the first time in my life, I had . . . nobody.

I lived it all ahead of time, there on the bathroom floor of our motel room.

This is ridiculous! I told myself. *You've got to get to sleep! Your only hope is to be up at five, crossing as much of the Mojave as possible before the arrival of the punishing sun. Pull yourself together. Get a grip!*

But I couldn't. I felt as if all the desert demons were after me.

Noticing the Bible clutched in my hand, I realized I hadn't had time for the day's devotional. Almost mechanically, I opened it to my bookmark, skimming for the verses where I'd left off somewhere in Revelation. *Let's see . . . chapter 12,* I began to read. *Oh, yes, the woman and the dragon.* A familiar passage. A scene of dramatic rescue as the child was snatched up to God and to His throne.

I read on. "The woman fled into the desert to a place prepared for her by God, where she might be taken care of. . . ." I sat up straight, my heart pounding. *The woman fled into the desert to a place prepared for her by God.*

In a very real sense, I was a woman in flight myself. Looking for a safe place, fleeing into the desert. The words were alive for me, as if I were hearing, not reading them.

Could it be that I wasn't alone? That my heavenly Father was already out there, in that frightening landscape, preparing a place for me?

In a twinkling, the desert was no longer a sinister threat to our safety but a haven to be embraced. The fear in my throat dissipated slowly as I sat there, eyes closed, beside the toilet, embracing the open Bible.

In a short while, I too, had settled for the night and was fast asleep.

My nerves were steady when the alarm went off. I got the kids up, fixed breakfast from the cooler and loaded up. It would be a long day, sixteen hours behind the wheel. I was grateful for the reassurance I'd received the night before. It didn't feel as immediate this morning, but I wanted to believe that the desert was somewhere that I might "be taken care of." I took a deep breath, and off we went.

We drove in the dark for a cool hour. Then the sun rose full throttle. Not a cloud to be seen. Or another car, for that matter. I looked at the dash, checking dials and gauges one more time. Temperature was holding okay, but my palms were getting a little sweaty.

I laid the back of my hand against the windshield. Hot already! *Thank You, Lord, for the air conditioning! Please, keep our little car going. Please take care of us* ... A place prepared for her by God, where she might be taken care of. ... I turned the words over again in my heart.

Almost subconsciously at first, I became aware that a shadow had fallen over the car. No matter the bends and curves in the road, the shadow bent and curved with us. The sky was perfectly blue and clear, except for this one little cloud whose shadow tracked our vehicle like a homing device.

After a couple of hours, we stopped at the one gasoline oasis in that vast expanse. I could see the cloud, like a patient friend, waiting for us at the highway. We resumed our journey, and the shadow cocooned us once more. Under its protection we traveled for another two hours. I relaxed. I laughed out loud with delight at the One Who was taking care of me.

As the highway tunneled us back into civilization, our cloud became one of many. It disappeared without me even being aware of it. But its presence remained with me, from that day to this. For I know that I dwell in a place prepared for me, so that I may be taken care of. And I am no longer afraid.

Surely he has done great things.
Be not afraid, O land;
be glad and rejoice.
Surely the LORD has done great things.
Be not afraid, O wild animals,
for the open pastures are becoming green.
The trees are bearing their fruit;
the fig tree and the vine yield their riches.
Be glad, O people of Zion,
rejoice in the LORD your God,
for he has given you
the autumn rains in righteousness.
He sends you abundant showers,
both autumn and spring rains, as before.
The threshing floors will be filled with grain;
the vats will overflow with new wine and oil. . . .
"You will have plenty to eat, until you are full,
and you will praise the name of the LORD your God,
who has worked wonders for you;
never again will my people be shamed."

—Joel 2:20–24, 26 (NIV)

Seeking God's Protection
Prayers in Times of Peril

CHAPTER 3
"LORD, SAVE ME!"

CHAPTER 4
"LORD, BE WITH MY CHILD"

Chapter 3 "Lord, Save Me!"

ord, save me!" These are the succinct and to-the-point words of Peter when he suddenly had second thoughts about walking on the water. You remember the story: Peter and the other disciples got caught in a storm in their boat on the lake. The wind was whipping up the waves against the boat, and they were terrified. When they saw Jesus walking toward them on the water, they thought they were seeing a ghost, until He called out to reassure them. Peter, who was always one to take the extra step (so to speak), challenged Jesus: "If that's really you, tell me to come to you on the water." When Jesus issued His invitation, Peter stepped out of the boat and began walking toward Jesus, until he looked around and saw the waves. That's when the fear set in and Peter cried out for help as he began sinking in the water. And then Jesus reached out, grabbed Peter's hand and helped him back into the boat.

Could there be a better story about God's help when we find ourselves in danger? We often find ourselves in situations when all we have time to say is "Lord, save me!" It doesn't matter how we managed to get into trouble or what kind of danger we're facing; we call out for help and God answers us, saying clearly, "I am here to help when you call on me." Intuitively and from experience, we know that when we face danger of any kind, all we need to do is call out to God and ask for help. These stories of God's extraordinary intervention remind us that He rescues us from danger and shelters us from harm.

"Lord, Save"

From the storms of the night
From dark ocean's wave
From the billowing crest
From the watery grave
Save us, Lord, save.
From tempests that roar
From the hurricane's rave
From the rock-strewn shore
From things that deprave
Save us, Lord, save.

—Celtic prayer

UNSEEN HANDS

KELSEY TYLER

I t was Christmas 1988, and the Moffitt family had shared a wonderful holiday together at their home in central Arizona. In addition to their presents, the family felt thankful for things that could not be wrapped and placed under a tree. Brian was very happy in his job as a local resort manager, and Ann was four months pregnant with their third child. Their first two, Erica, five, and Brianna, four, were healthy and happy and the source of much joy. In fact, the Moffitt family couldn't have been happier.

After celebrating Christmas at home that year, the family climbed into their Toyota Landcruiser and headed for Payson, Arizona—a small town about ninety minutes away. Since Brian's parents lived in Payson, he knew the roads well and enjoyed the scenic drive.

"It never gets old, does it?" Brian asked his wife, reaching over to hold her hand as they climbed toward Payson. "God sure knows how to make things beautiful."

Ann smiled and placed his hand on her pregnant abdomen. "He sure does."

The visit with Brian's parents was fun-filled and full of the laughter of Erica and Brianna, but after two days it was time to return home. A light snow was falling as they packed up the Landcruiser and said their good-byes.

"I hate to drive in snow," Ann said as they climbed in and buckled their seat belts.

"I know," Brian said calmly. "But you're not driving, I am. And I'm perfectly fine with it. Just say a prayer that we get home safely."

Ann nodded and silently asked God to guard their car as they drove home. That done, she did her best not to worry. She stared out her window and admitted that the snow was certainly beautiful. It fell gently and looked like freshly sifted powdered sugar on the ground.

Highway 260, the road that leads from Payson to the Verde Valley where the Moffitts lived, is a two-lane road with an occasional passing lane. From Brian's parents' house the highway climbs slightly until it reaches the small towns of Strawberry and Pine, and then it continues downhill for nearly forty minutes until leveling out in the Verde Valley.

Although traffic was light that morning, Brian drove slowly and carefully, aware that there were patches of ice under the snow-covered road. Most of the cars on the road had snow chains on their tires, and though the Moffitts did not, they felt secure in four-wheel drive and that the Landcruiser had heavy-duty snow tires.

Still, Brian sensed his wife's fears as they began the section of highway that was nearly straight downhill. He glanced at his wife and smiled warmly. "Honey, it'll be okay. Don't worry."

"I know, I know," Ann said. "I just wish we were home, that's all."

"We'll be home soon. Try to relax."

Ann nodded, but she could feel a tension throughout her body. The road seemed especially slippery, despite the fact that Brian was driving in a low gear.

Just as the highway became steep, Brian shifted into yet a lower gear just to be sure they wouldn't lose traction. Suddenly the back of the Landcruiser began fishtailing across the road, swinging from one side of the highway to the other. Brian struggled to correct the truck's steering, but as he turned the wheel, he could feel that it was having no effect on the tires. Suddenly he knew what had happened. The vehicle was in a slide with the tires completely detached from the road.

At that instant the Landcruiser swung sharply toward oncoming traffic, sending the vehicle spinning in a complete circle.

"Oh, Jesus!" Ann screamed, grabbing on to the dashboard. "In the name of Jesus, please stop!"

The Landcruiser stopped spinning and began a fast sideways slide toward the cliff that buttressed the edge of the highway. If the vehicle slid off the road, Brian and Ann knew they would probably be killed since the fall would send them several hundred feet down the hill along rough terrain.

"Jesus, please help us!" Ann screamed again. But deep in her heart she knew they were traveling too fast and felt certain that they were going over the edge.

Then just before the drop-off, the Landcruiser slammed to a sudden stop. One of the girls had taken off her seat belt and the harsh jolt sent the child flying across the car into the window.

For a moment there was silence.

Brian looked at his wife in shock, not believing that they had avoided going over the edge of the highway. He was amazed that they were alive.

"Girls, are you okay?" he asked, turning around.

"Yes, Daddy," came a small voice. "I hit my head, but I'm okay."

Relieved, Brian stared at his wife once more. "We must have hit a tree stump or a boulder or something," he said.

"Maybe a guardrail," Ann added.

Still shaky from the closeness of what could have been a deadly car accident, Brian climbed out of the truck. He walked around the vehicle to the side that was not parallel with the cliff. "What did we hit?" she asked.

"That's just it. We didn't hit anything. There's not a rock or a piece of wood, no guardrail. Nothing. The truck just stopped for no reason at all."

Ann examined the edge of the road and saw that Brian was right. The truck had been sliding at more than ten-miles-per-hour and had suddenly stopped for no explainable reason. Together they looked down the jagged, rocky mountainside and shuddered at the thought of what might have happened.

"Ann, it's like the hand of God just reached out and stopped us from going over the mountainside."

Quietly Ann remembered her desperate plea for Jesus to help them. She reached over and circled her arms around her husband's waist, resting her head on his chest. "With all my heart I believe you're right. We were stopped by the hand of God. It must have been a miracle."

BEHIND ENEMY LINES

WALTER WALKER

n June of 1995, F-16 pilot Captain Scott O'Grady, along with thirty-four other pilots from the 555th Squadron of the United States Air Force's 31st Fighter Wing, was stationed at Aviano Air Base in northeastern Italy. Their mission was to enforce the NATO no-fly zone in the skies over Bosnia.

"BASHER 52," Captain O'Grady's call name, had already racked up forty-six "Deny Flight" sorties over Bosnia, four of them with his new wingman, Bob ("Wilbur") Wright. The objective for the June 2 mission was to back up U.N. peacekeepers on the ground and to prevent anyone—Serbs, Croats or Muslims—from using the air to project military power against the other warring factions. After more than a year of "Deny Flights" over Bosnia, hostile ground fire had taken down only one British Harrier. That pilot was returned on the same day by local Muslims. But things were now heating up. Three hundred fifty U.N. peacekeepers were being held hostage, and NATO had launched air strikes against Bosnian Serb munitions depots.

O'Grady and Wright were continuing their patrol after their first mid-air refueling, carefully avoiding the surface-to-air (SAM) threats. They had no way of knowing that the Bosnian Serbs had secretly tractored an SA-6 SAM battery right into the path of their patrol.

At exactly 3:03 P.M., O'Grady's alarm went off indicating that he was being tracked by acquisition radar. Six seconds later a louder alarm went off, signaling that he had been locked onto by target-tracking radar, the type of radar that guides a missile, and which was probably already on its way. The words "COUNTER, COUNTER" squawked in his headset. O'Grady began to negotiate maneuvers that would push the F-16 to its limits. Three seconds later an SA-6 missile exploded between the two planes. O'Grady's plane was cut in two by a direct belly hit.

Having just refueled, his F-16 was like a flying gas tank. Surrounded by fire, Captain O'Grady found the lever located between his legs and ejected himself from the plane, traveling three hundred-fifty miles per hour at twenty-six thousand feet.

As he floated down from twenty-four thousand feet, where he had manually opened the parachute, O'Grady could see soldiers in trucks arriving to capture their prize. He had no idea, if captured, whether he would be tortured, killed or held hostage.

O'Grady came down only a short distance from troops searching for him. Releasing the parachute harness, he began moving as fast as he could away from them.

For the next five days Captain O'Grady evaded detection as he tried unsuccessfully to make radio contact with friendly forces. On the first day, two men walked up to the very edge of his hiding spot. They almost stepped on him. "I don't know why they missed me," O'Grady commented later, "can't explain it, except that God veiled me from them."

O'Grady prayed continually. "In Bosnia I caught a glimpse of God's love, and it was the most incredible experience of my life. I'd tapped into the brightest, most joyous feeling; I felt warmed by an everlasting flame. For all my physical complaints, I'd been on a spiritual high since that missile and I intersected."

On two occasions during the days he was evading the Bosnian Serbs, O'Grady had something of a divine encounter:

> *The enemy chopper left my vicinity after fifteen minutes . . .*
> *And then I shut my eyes, and something happened to make*
> *me realize that I wasn't outnumbered, after all—that I*
> *had more allies than I could count. I prayed, and I wasn't*
> *a solo. I had joined a huge chorus; I could hear prayers for*
> *me from throughout the world, from my family to the most*
> *remote, faceless stranger. There were no barriers of lan-*
> *guage, or politics, or even religion. There was only a rising*
> *tide of unity, and caring, and belief.*

On his third day of hiding O'Grady was praying again:

> *Before long I felt a definite presence. It grew more and more vivid, until I could see it, shimmering in my mind's eye. It's hard to put this into words, but I saw the vision through feeling it, and the feeling was very warm and good. That international chorus welled up again, praying for my safe return. I can't tell you how important that vision was to me. It gave me the courage to go on.*

After completing his own mission, Captain Thomas Hanford, a veteran fighter pilot from the 510th Fighter Squadron, remained in Bosnian airspace to the very limits of his fuel reserves, continuing to search for O'Grady's radio beacon. On June 8, he picked up O'Grady's faint signal. Within hours, a rescue force made up of more than forty aircraft and scores of Marines was on its way to extract O'Grady.

Several days later Captain O'Grady arrived at Andrews Air Force Base aboard an Air Force C-20. Getting off the plane, he particularly noticed the big banner:

BASHER 52

America's Been Praying

Welcome Home

Scott O'Grady

DIVINE FIRE INSULATION

JOAN WESTER ANDERSON

Like Joe, Richard Tomasello, a lieutenant in the Scranton, Pennsylvania, Fire Department, has never considered himself a hero. He would tell you that climbing into burning buildings, rescuing people, and sometimes running out of oxygen are things that just go with the job. But he does his share of praying just the same. And, like Joe, he knows that God can move air and space whenever He wishes to do so.

One day in January 1997, Richard's engine company was called to a house engulfed in flames. "There's someone in there," one of the men called to Richard.

"I'm going in!" he responded.

Richard searched the bedrooms first, but no one was in there. "Then I turned to enter another room, and the full blast of the fire hit me," he recalls. The explosion was so strong that it knocked Richard's helmet off. And there was no hose line of water there!

He had to get out immediately. "I broke the windowpanes out around me. I could barely see them through the smoke. And when the glass fell, someone below ran and got a ladder and also threw a hose up to me," he says. The fire was roaring now, much too strong to be put out with just one thin stream of water, so Richard kept wetting down the area around him, in hopes of keeping the approaching flames from burning him. Then his oxygen-tank alarm went off. Only a few minutes of air left.

"I backed up to the window and tried to get through it," Richard recalls. "There was no chance. It was a really small opening, and I was way too big for it." Richard pushed, pulled, squeezed and wriggled, while continuing to wet the flames now licking at his coat, but there was no possibility of escape. He was going to be burned alive, right there, right then. If he didn't die of smoke inhalation first.

No. He wouldn't go so easily. "God, please help," he whispered, then stuck his head through the minuscule opening again. This time he perceived something that had not been there before. It was a touch, all around him, that he could feel but not see. A circular barrier between him and the dangerous heat and flames. Now he was being lifted, now going right through the window!

Richard came out of the opening headfirst, grabbed the top of the ladder and made his way down to the street. His fellow firefighters stared at him in astonishment. They had been getting ready to go up and get him, they explained, but were taking another route. How had he gotten through that tiny window?

When they took the ladder down, they had another surprise. The top few rungs were completely burned. The flames had obviously leaped out the window while

Richard was trying to get out of it. Richard's white lieutenant shirt collar, sticking out from under his protective coat, was entirely black too.

Yet, although his helmet had fallen off and the flames had been all around him, he had no burns—nor any soot—on his head or face. It was as if he had been enfolded in powerful, protective arms. The situation seemed impossible. And yet it had happened.

Richard's wife, Joanne, had the answer when he related the story to her that night. "It was a miracle," she said simply. And why not?

CAPSIZED!

DEBRA LAUGHLIN

Visitors flock to North Carolina beaches every year, and in the spring of 1997, the Camarerros were no exception. German and Oliva, the parents of our fifteen-year-old Spanish exchange student, also named Oliva, had come from Madrid, Spain, for a two-week visit with their daughter, and the beach was high on their list of must-see stops. So one unseasonably warm spring day, I took my two children, John, seven, and Emily, three, and the Camarerros to visit my parents at their beach home in Aydlett, North Carolina, about fifty miles from where we lived. The eight of us decided to take advantage of the beautiful weather by donning our swimsuits and boarding my father's twenty-foot, Coast Guard-approved deck boat to head across Currituck Sound to the unspoiled beaches of Corolla, a remote barrier island resort, for fun in the sun. After a twenty-minute boat ride there, we explored Corolla's lighthouse, gathered seashells and took advantage of some great photo opportunities.

After about an hour, we felt hungry. German had promised to make us Spanish paella for lunch, so we boarded the boat and set sail for home. Although the wind had picked up some since we'd arrived, no one was worried; the weather forecast had been fine. Yet the waters of the Sound seemed choppier; sprays of water whipped at the boat's hull, bouncing upward and soaking us.

It's going to be a long, wet ride home, I thought. I had no idea how right I was.

As we approached the middle of the Sound, dark clouds filled the sky. Winds began topping at forty miles per hour, while waves crested at three to four feet. Since my father's a seasoned boater, at first I wasn't too concerned. But as our boat struggled in the water, a sense of foreboding overtook me. Why was the motor working overtime—with so little progress against the pummeling waves and winds? Unbeknownst to us, the hull of my father's boat had cracked because of a manufacturer's defect, and water was pouring in.

As John and Emily huddled beside me, shivering, Oliva moved to the back to sit with her mother. Before long, waves cascaded over the back of the boat. John and Emily started crying; anxiety appeared on the Camarerros' faces, as well as my mom's. Since Oliva's parents spoke no English and we spoke no Spanish, I flashed them the "okay" sign to keep them calm. Then, fighting my own fear, I pulled my children close to me and breathed a quick prayer: "Lord, please see us through this."

Water started pouring in, overwhelming the boat's bilge pump. As I helped German bail out the water, I remembered a Bible verse I'd recently memorized: "When I am afraid, I will trust in you. In God, whose word I praise, in God I trust; I will not be afraid" (Psalm 56:3–4, NIV). I repeated it as I frantically bailed the last of the water out of the tossing boat. Just as I caught my breath, I noticed the boat was listing to the right.

"Dad!" I yelled, "The boat is leaning!"

My father immediately lifted the hatch and saw the equivalent of two thousand gallons of water in the hull. He quickly handed out life jackets and commanded everyone to get into the center of the boat in an attempt to stabilize it.

"Get your jackets on, we're going into the water!" he shouted. I couldn't believe it.

"No, Dad, no!" I shouted back. "You can fix anything!"

"Debbie, it's over," my dad said with quiet reserve. At that, our exchange student, Oliva, became hysterical. John cried, "Mommy, I don't want to die!" Emily just screamed. This must be a very bad dream, I told myself.

As the boat leaned to the left, we shifted to the right like little crabs. But the motion of the water in the hull, the waves and the wind, were too much for the crippled vessel. I grabbed Emily's hand as well as an extra life jacket, and we crept to the top of the boat—Titaniclike—to delay the inevitable: being plunged, slow-motion, into the salty, fifty-degree water. When the boat capsized, my dad hit the water first. I lost sight of John. Emily and I were tossed in the cold, dark water; it felt as though I'd landed on a thousand knives. The water consumed me like a large monster. As I fought my way to the surface, separated from Emily, I knew instantly she'd gotten trapped under the boat. I dove under to rescue Emily, but when we emerged, my life-jacket cord caught on some underwater object. I couldn't get to the surface. I panicked. Instead of thinking to unsnap and untie, I frantically ripped at my jacket and desperately tried to reach the surface. Finally, miraculously, whatever held me under released its hold—and I was free.

On the surface, there was pandemonium—screaming and crying. A small piece of boat remained floating and my mother, John, Emily, Oliva and her mom scrambled on top, coughing and choking on the salty water. My dad frantically did a quick head count as he floated in the rough, frigid water with German and me: eight. We were all there. But despite my life jacket, I was floundering. Just six weeks earlier, another boating tragedy on the same body of water had claimed four other lives, two of whom were children. Here we are, facing the same untimely death, I thought. This is how we're going to die.

No one else was boating that day. No one knew we were boating. We had no flares. We had no radio. No rescue was imminent. I knew I was a strong swimmer— I'd been a lifeguard in high school—so when I asked my mother out of desperation if I should try to swim to shore, she said, "Yes! Go!"

As I headed toward mainland, German insisted he join me. Within minutes we lost sight of the boat. Even though we both had life jackets, waves continually pulled us under. When we'd resurface another wave would pummel us back down. Although German and I tried to stay together, the wind and waves separated us. We called out until we found each other again and resumed the treacherous journey.

At one point, I started to choke on seawater and panic rose in my throat. I knew if I let it out, it would consume me. German swam over to me, grabbed me, and said firmly, "No, no, Debra! *Tranquila, tranquila!*" (the Spanish word for calm).

We'd been into our swim about an hour and a half when I started growing weary and cold. As my legs cramped, I began to think I'd made a mistake by leaving the boat. Shore was still so far away. Because of the panic, I hadn't said good-bye to my children. I hadn't told them I loved them. I'd just swum away.

I also thought of my husband, John, a navy pilot deployed in the Persian Gulf. He'd have to come home and bury his family.

With every stroke I took, I said a prayer. I mentally recited every Bible verse and sang every hymn I could remember. I begged God for mercy; I begged him for strength. I begged him for my children's lives. I prayed, "God, please, please, please see us through this!"

Back on the boat, John and Emily huddled between my mom and Oliva. My father remained in the water, holding onto a rope tied to the boat. It had been three hours since German and I'd left, and they were beginning to despair. My father started to cry, telling my mom he was sorry. He felt it was his fault; he also told her he thought German and I had been gone too long; he was certain we were dead. My dad tied himself to the wreckage, telling my mom not to untie him. He didn't want to float around for days, dead and undiscovered.

But what my father didn't know was that German and I did make it, just as the sun was setting—two and a half hours after we first set out. We hit shore at 4:30 P.M. and flagged down a cyclist, who alerted the neighbors. German and I were carried into a neighbor's home, then treated for hypothermia at the Coast Guard station.

Within minutes, the shore was filled with police, rescue workers, and the Coast Guard, who sent out their rescue helicopter.

Fifteen-year-old Oliva was the first to spot the helicopter. She pointed and cried, "Helicopter! Helicopter!" Every one on the boat began to cry and wave their arms in the air. First the helicopter circled, then dropped a rescue swimmer in the water with a basket. All six were safely airlifted out of the water and taken to the Elizabeth City Coast Guard Station, where we were reunited.

One hour later, the boat sank. Nine days later, it washed to shore.

Three weeks later, I returned to my parents' beach house. My dad had retrieved the remains of the boat; it was devastating to see the wreckage. I visited the pier where German and I were pulled from the water. Currituck Sound looked calm and beautiful. As I stood on the pier and looked over what could have been our watery grave, I noticed a twelve-foot cross to the right of the pier. It had been erected for

Easter Sunday; I hadn't noticed it the day of the accident because I was so distraught. Suddenly I felt overwhelmed by the presence of God and awed by how my prayers for survival had been answered. . . .

Recently our pastor talked about being thankful. "Can you thank God for an experience, even if you never know why it happened?" he asked us. At the time of the boating accident, I couldn't fathom why it was happening. As a new Christian, I didn't feel ready to die, or for my children to die. But now I know God was teaching me about His glory and faithfulness.

An extraordinary event? Yes. A supernatural work of God? I believe so. Today I celebrate life—and thank God for giving us each new day!

VOICE FROM THE TOWER

KELSEY TYLER

David Moore had never flown before, but that Sunday night in July 1971, when he was offered the opportunity to fly from Texas to North Carolina to see his wife and infant daughter, David didn't hesitate.

"What time do we leave?" he asked his friend, Henry Gardner. The man was a local crop duster and he owned a small Cessna 180. He had planned to take a sight-seeing trip the next day, and was willing to go out of his way to see that David and his family were reunited. The past nine weeks had been especially traumatic for the Moore family, and Gardner wanted to do what he could to help.

The trouble began when David, twenty-four, and his wife Florence, twenty-one, discovered that her mother was dying of cancer. The sick woman lived in Hendersonville, North Carolina—at least a two-day drive from Yoakum, Texas, where the young couple and their infant daughter lived. The situation was especially difficult because David had recently been named pastor of Hebron Baptist Church, a position which required his presence—especially on Sundays.

"We'll work out a schedule," David assured his wife, "so that we can spend as much time as possible in North Carolina."

The staff at Hebron Baptist was completely understanding and arranged for David to take a partial leave of absence. As long as Florence's mother was ill, David could be gone during the week and then home for the Sunday morning service.

The couple decided that Florence and their daughter would stay in North Carolina while David drove the weekly commute to Texas. Nine times David made the round-trip trek before he began feeling the strain of the routine.

"I need to rest," he admitted to Florence one evening as he was preparing to return to Texas once again.

"Honey, why don't you take the bus?" She was worried about his long hours on the road. "That way you can sleep, or catch up on your plans for Sunday, and it won't be so hard on you."

David thought for a moment, "Good idea," he said, rubbing his tired eyes. "And you could have the car so you'd have some way to get around if you need to."

He boarded a passenger bus late that week determined to spend the next two days resting. Instead the trip was a nightmarish forty-six hours of crying babies, constant stops and loud conversations. His family was on a tight budget, and he could not afford to fly. But David was more exhausted than ever before, and he decided he'd rather walk back to North Carolina, or hitchhike the highways than ride another bus for two straight days.

Over the weekend, Henry Gardner's daughter—a member of Hebron Baptist Church—caught wind of David's need to find a way back to North Carolina. She told her father, and on Sunday night, Henry called with his offer.

"It's a small plane, but smooth as honey in the air," Henry said. "You can be my navigator."

In the recesses of his mind, David felt a slight wave of anxiety course through his body. He had always been wary of small planes, and expected that when the time came for him to fly, it would be on a jumbo jet. He pushed aside his momentary fears and cleared his throat.

"I've never done any navigating," he said with a laugh. "But I'd be willing to fly the plane myself if it meant getting back to my family."

David met Henry the next day at a small airport outside town. The morning was beautiful, clear and without any trace of bad weather.

"Looks like we picked a good day to hit the skies." Henry said, easily shifting his body into the cockpit.

David sized up the tiny aircraft and silently, almost unconsciously, whispered a prayer: *Lord, guide us as we go and please get us there safely.*

For the first half hour the craft flew easily through the clear skies, but as they neared Houston, they entered a thick fog.

"No problem," Henry said, pointing out the windshield. "You can see the Houston radio towers there above the fog. If we keep our eyes on them, we'll know where we are. Besides, we have aviation maps on board. Everything will be fine."

For a while, it looked as if Henry would be right. Then, when the plane was just outside Jackson, Mississippi, the fog worsened so that the plane became cocooned in a cloud with no visibility whatsoever.

Almost at the same time, the plane's radio and instruments died. Suddenly, the men could no longer see anything on the ground, and because of the instrument failure, they couldn't monitor the fuel or talk to people in the control tower.

David may have been inexperienced at flying but he did not need a pilot's license to know that they were in grave danger. His thoughts turned to his pretty young wife and their sixteen-month-old daughter. The couple was in the process of adopting the child, and they were expecting to sign the final papers any time. *Please, God, help us,* he prayed silently, his hands clenched and his face white with terror. *Please get us through safely.*

At that moment, they flew through a clearing in the fog and caught a glimpse of the small Jackson airport just below. Henry maneuvered the craft through the opening in the clouds and smoothly came down onto the runway.

"Thank God," David whispered as the men climbed out of the plane and Henry began tinkering with the fuse box. A burned-out fuse had caused the instrument failure and Henry replaced it while David telephoned Florence.

"Listen, honey," David told Florence, "we're running late because of bad weather. Meet me at the Asheville Airport about an hour later than we planned."

"Is everything okay? With the plane, I mean?" she asked. David could hear how Florence was trying to control the concern in her voice.

"It's fine," he said sounding more confident than he felt. "I love you, honey. See you in a few hours."

As they climbed back in the craft, David again uttered a silent prayer: *You got us this far, God. Please see us through safely to North Carolina.*

In less than an hour the men were back in the sky enjoying the fact that the sun had come out and the conditions were once again clear. By the time they flew over Atlanta, Georgia, David's fears had nearly disappeared and he began looking forward to being with his family.

Then, as the plane passed Greenville, South Carolina, the fog appeared once more and almost instantly engulfed the small craft in a dense, suffocating blanket of gray. Moments later they approached a mountain range and David watched as Henry struggled to clear it safely.

"After these mountains, it should be sunny again," David said struggling to convince himself as much as Henry. "There's never fog in this area."

But that afternoon, there was indeed fog and it was so thick that the men could see nothing past the plane's windshield. The airport wasn't far away, and Henry immediately contacted the Asheville Airport for assistance.

"We're closed because of the fog," the air traffic controller informed Henry. "We have no capability for instrument landing. Return to Greenville and land there."

"I can't," Henry said, a tinge of panic creeping into his voice. "We're almost out of fuel. We don't have enough to fly back to Greenville."

For a moment, the cockpit was eerily silent. They had no visibility, and David's eyes fell on the fuel gauge and the needle which danced dangerously over the letter *E*. Again he silently prayed, struggling to control his terror: *Please, God, get us out of these clouds safely.*

Finally, a different voice broke the silence, "Okay. We'll get the ground crew ready. Come in on an emergency landing."

David clutched the sides of his seat, his eyes wide in disbelief. There was no way they could make an emergency landing when visibility between the plane and the control tower was completely cut off by the fog.

Henry's voice snapped David to attention.

"Get the aviation maps."

David opened them instantly, and Henry estimated their location. According to the map, they should be directly above the airport. Gradually, Henry began to descend through the fog toward the ground. As he did, the voice of the controller entered the cockpit.

"Pull it up! Pull it up!"

Henry responded immediately, just as both men saw a split in the fog. They were not over the airport as they had thought. Instead they were over a busy interstate highway, and had missed an overpass bridge by no more than five feet.

David felt his heart thumping wildly, and he was struck by the certainty of one thing. Short of divine intervention, there was no way they would escape their grave situation alive.

At that instant, the controller's voice broke the silence once again. "If you will listen to me, I'll help you get down," he said.

Henry released a pent up sigh. "Go ahead. I'm listening."

David closed his eyes momentarily and prayed, begging God to guide them safely through the fog onto the ground.

Meanwhile, the controller began guiding Henry toward a landing.

"Come down a little. Okay, a little more. Not that much. All right, now over to the right. Straighten it out and come down a little more."

The calm reassuring voice of the controller continued its steady stream of directions, and Henry, intent on the voice, did as he was instructed. The trip seemed to take an eternity, and David wondered whether he would see his wife and daughter again. "Please, God," he whispered. "Get us onto the ground, God. Please."

The controller continued. "Raise it a little more. Okay, you're too far to the left.

That's right. Now lower it a little more. All right, you're right over the end of the runway. Set it down. Now!"

Carefully responding just as he was told, Henry lowered the plane, and when he was a few feet from the ground the runway came into sight. As the plane touched down, David saw Florence standing nearby waiting for him, and his eyes filled with tears of relief and gratitude.

The two men looked at each other and without saying a word, they bowed their heads and closed their eyes. "Thank You, God," David said, his voice choked with emotion. "Thank you for sparing our lives today. And thank you for listening."

Henry picked up the plane's radio and contacted the control tower. "Hey, I just want to thank you so much for what you did. We couldn't have made it without those directions. You probably saved our lives."

There was a brief pause. "What are you talking about?" the controller asked. He had a different voice this time, and he was clearly confused. "We lost all radio contact with you when we told you to return to Greenville."

Goose bumps rose up on David's arms, and he watched as Henry's face went blank in disbelief. "You *what?*" He asked.

"We never heard from you again and we never heard you talking to us or to anyone else," the controller said. "We were stunned when we saw you break through the clouds right over the runway. It was a perfect landing."

David and Henry looked at each other in a way that needed no words. If the Asheville controller hadn't been in contact with them through the emergency landing, who had? Whose calm clear voice had filled the cockpit with the directions that saved their lives?

> I waited patiently for the LORD;
> he turned to me and heard my cry.
> He lifted me out of the slimy pit,
> out of the mud and mire;
> he set my feet on a rock
> and gave me a firm place to stand.
> He put a new song in my mouth,
> a hymn of praise to our God.
> Many will see and fear
> and put their trust in the LORD. . . .
> Many, O LORD my God,
> are the wonders you have done.
> The things you planned for us
> no one can recount to you;
> were I to speak and tell of them,
> they would be too many to declare.

—Psalm 40:1–3, 5 (NIV)

Chapter 4   *"Lord, Be with My Child"*

There is probably no instinct stronger than the instinct to protect our children. We seek to keep them safe from their own recklessness, from those who would prey on them, from the dangers of traffic and stairs, unfriendly dogs and bacteria. We would endure their pain ourselves if we could, but we also realize that risk is a part of life, and if children don't take risks, then they will not mature. How can they learn to avoid danger for themselves if they never face the consequences of their own decisions? This is the exquisite balance of parenting.

Most parents thank God for their children and seek His love and protection for them on a daily basis. These prayers are as natural as breathing—and as regular. We see many examples of them in the Bible: Hannah, Mary, Zachariah, their prayers a part of our daily worship. But when a child faces a threat, we marshal every weapon we have to protect them, and that includes prayer. Our prayers for our children are probably the most primitive prayers we pray, pouring from our deepest soul. They are stark, spontaneous, direct, excruciating. And these prayers are effective.

As we read these stories, we are reminded that our loving Father understands the love we have for our children and responds to our pleadings on their behalf.

"For Our Children"

Father, hear us, we are praying,
Hear the words our hearts are saying,
We are praying for our children.
Keep them from the power of evil,
From secret hidden peril,
From the whirlpool that would suck them,
From the treacherous quicksand, pluck them.
From the worldling's hollow gladness,
From the sting of faithless sadness,
Holy Father, save our children.
Through life's troubled water steer them,
Through life's bitter battle cheer them,
Father, Father, be Thou near them.
Read the language of our longing,
Read the wordless pleadings thronging,
And wherever they may bide,
Lead them home at eventide.

—Amy Carmichael

DANGER IN THE CANYON

ANDREA GROSS

As Shirley Halliday unlocked the door to her home in Hartland, Michigan, she realized she was truly alone for the first time in her adult life. Three months earlier, in May 1976, her husband had died. Now her thirteen-year-old daughter, Janie, the youngest of her six children and the only one still living at home, was away on vacation with one of her older brothers.

Shirley, a nurse, had just finished working the night shift at the hospital. As she prepared for her morning devotion, a strange feeling came over her. She knew—absolutely *knew*—that Janie was in danger. An icy cold swept over her and wrenching sobs shook her body.

Meanwhile, more than fifteen hundred miles away, Janie had wandered away from her brother and sister-in-law, fascinated by her first view of the Painted Desert. Standing at the top of a ravine so deep she couldn't see the bottom, she thought the Arizona landscape looked like something from another world. She stepped over the low guardrail to get a better view—and lost her footing.

Tumbling down the sloping canyon walls, Janie frantically tried to grab onto something, anything to slow her descent, but the rock was weathered and slippery, and the sand that covered it offered almost no traction. Janie began sliding faster and faster, swept toward certain death.

Back in Michigan, Shirley, in desperation, called on the angels to save her daughter. Aloud, she read Psalm 91:11–12 (NKJV): "For He shall give His angels charge over you, to keep you in all your ways. They shall bear you up in their hands, lest you dash your foot against a stone." As the family later reconstructed the scene, it was at the exact moment when Shirley finished her prayers that Janie miraculously slid to a stop, fifty yards from where she had fallen.

Her face white and her hands scraped from grabbing at the rocky cliff, Janie looked around. What had halted her? There were no protrusions in the canyon wall or clumps of vegetation to break her fall. It was as if an invisible hand had reached across her path and caught her.

With no help in sight, the dazed girl slowly inched her way back up by sitting down and pushing herself backward, ignoring the dirt and gravel embedded in her legs and the smashed camera in her back pocket. As Janie reached the top—where her frantic relatives would soon find her—Shirley felt overwhelmed by a great sense of peace. She knew her daughter was safe now.

Both Janie, now twenty-nine and an interior designer, and Shirley, who has since remarried, are still awed by what they believe is a miracle. "From that moment I knew that the Lord watches over the widow and is father to the fatherless," says Shirley. "I had no fear about raising my youngest child alone because I was confident that I had the help of God and His angels."

VITAL SIGNS

JOAN WESTER ANDERSON

When Emily Weichman was seven months old, she had a stroke. Although the episode had never been repeated, Emily was still delicate, and her mother, Marlene, watched her carefully for signs of illness or distress. And so did the members of the Weichmans' church community, St. Paul Lutheran in West Point, Nebraska. "Emily has many adoptive grandparents," Marlene says. "Everyone is concerned about her."

In September 1991, Marlene, her husband, and Emily, then five, decided to accompany Marlene's parents to Seattle to visit relatives. On the way home, they stayed overnight at a campsite in Yellowstone National Park.

The following morning Emily seemed lethargic, and after they got on the road she quickly fell asleep again. The family was driving through a desolate stretch of Wyoming when Emily abruptly awoke.

"Mommy," she said, "I'm sick." Marlene looked at her daughter. Emily's eyes seemed out of focus, shifting to the right. A moment later she started vomiting.

They had just driven over some road oil. Were fumes nauseating Emily? Marlene's father stopped the RV, and everyone walked her up and down. She was conscious and apparently aware, but Marlene, a teacher, had had epileptic students, and she felt a chill of apprehension. Emily's symptoms seemed ominously similar. "Dad," she said, "we've got to get Emily to a hospital right away!"

The nearest town, Rock Springs, was over sixty miles away. Marlene's father sped off, and everyone began to pray.

Twenty miles, thirty. . . . The scenery flew by, but not quickly enough. Emily seemed to be fading. Everyone kept praying, but as they approached Rock Springs, they could see that the town below was far larger than they had anticipated. There would certainly be a hospital here, but how would they find it? Precious moments would be lost as they searched. Emily was unconscious now. "Lord," Marlene whispered as she held her daughter tightly, "we need to find a doctor fast."

Just as they approached an interstate highway, everyone saw a blue marker with a white *H* on it—a hospital sign! Thank God! Soon they saw another. At least four signs formed a reassuring blue-and-white trail, which Marlene's father followed on and off the interstate, right to the hospital.

An emergency-room physician diagnosed Emily's condition as a mild epileptic seizure, did a CAT scan and quickly stabilized her with anticonvulsant drugs.

Only afterward, as Emily rested safely in her room, did Marlene feel the full impact of the crisis. "If it weren't for those hospital signs," she told the physician, "we might still be driving around."

The doctor looked at her curiously. "What signs?"

"The ones lining our route," Marlene explained. "They were literally a lifesaver. We couldn't have found the hospital without them."

The doctor was perplexed. "I live about eight miles out on that road. I travel it every day here," he told her. "I've never seen any hospital signs."

Marlene didn't know what to think. All four adults in the van had seen the markers. But her father and her husband were now at a gas station they had passed on the way in, having the RV checked out. When they returned, she'd ask them.

The men returned late because they had gotten lost. "We were counting on those blue-and-white signs to guide us," her father said. "But they were gone."

Still perplexed, Marlene phoned the Rock Springs Chamber of Commerce the next day. But an official could provide no explanation. "There have never been any hospital signs along that route." he said.

With the help of anticonvulsant drugs, Emily is stable and happy today, and considered a "miracle child" among the members of St. Paul, many of whom make it a point to travel that same road whenever they can. There's no doubt it's holy ground.

ANOTHER SLEEPLESS NIGHT

DONNA WEBER

I do not fall asleep easily; I never have. Night after night I lie awake next to my husband, Louis, as he sleeps. Sometimes I review the events of the day in my mind, going over small things that happened at work, or thinking about larger things going on in the world around me. Often I think about my three children. And when I do finally fall asleep, my mind is filled with vivid dreams. One of those dreams woke me up one night, and as it turns out, it was for a very good reason.

Scott was my middle child. He was a delightful child, very independent and capable. Our family spent a great deal of time with one another when the children were young; we liked nothing better than a good long camping trip together at our lake lot or at other neighboring lakes. Scott was a master camper, very sure of himself in the woods, in the water and with our small boat.

It was clear during his high school years that he would probably not go on to college, and his father and I hoped Scott would find his way toward a trade he could master. When he announced his intention of joining the Air Force after graduation, we couldn't have been more pleased. Louis had been in the Air Force, too, and was proud that his son planned to follow in his footsteps. True to Scott's independent nature, he took the bus on his own the two hundred and thirty miles from our town of Aberdeen to Sioux Falls for his physical. I worried that he was too young to be off on his own, but he had other ideas.

Years later, I worried again when he announced that he planned to live in Alaska. Alaska? So far from home in South Dakota? But Scott was determined and excited about his new life in Alaska, and I gradually put my fears aside. It turns out that Alaska is not really so far from South Dakota—we've visited there four times now, and I understand why my son has such love for that beautiful state. A devoted outdoorsman, Scott carries on the camping traditions our family started in his childhood.

And that was Scott's life in Alaska up until the night I had my dream. As I try to recall the circumstances of that night, I can't remember too many details of the dream. All I know is that I was suddenly awake in the middle of the night with a terrible fear about Scott's safety. Louis slept soundly as I lay there in bed, my heart racing. My child was in danger, I just knew it!

He needed my help. How could I help my son in Alaska from my bedroom in South Dakota? There was only one answer: I could pray.

I climbed quietly out of bed and knelt down next to it. I prayed for God to protect my son Scott, to keep him safe and deliver him from harm. I prayed for just a short while, pleading over and over for Scott's life. At last, emotionally drained, I climbed back into bed.

A day or two afterward, I received a call from Scott's former wife, who was in Alaska. "Donna, I need to tell you about something that's happened to Scott. He is in the hospital recovering from a plane crash that happened out in the wilderness." She assured me that he was stable, that I didn't need to bother to come. But once again, I felt that I should be there.

A few days later, we stood next to my injured son's hospital bed. As he grew stronger he was able to tell me the details of what had happened: While he and his friend Gary were returning from a moose hunting trip in the wilderness, their plane was caught upon takeoff by a wind shear. The plane skidded on its belly to a stop and burst into flames. Although Gary had been able to climb out quickly, Scott's seat belt buckle had jammed. As he frantically tried to free himself, he suddenly felt a powerful hand on his shoulder assisting him. Finally free and able to get a safe distance away from the plane, Scott turned to thank Gary for saving him. "Save you?" Gary replied, "I was thirty feet away, rolling on the ground. I never went near the plane!"

I was amazed and humbled. While my son was trapped in a burning plane I had sent him the only help I could: a mother's prayers. Although it would take many months of painful treatment before Scott's injuries were fully healed, he credits the love and support of his family and friends with helping him through the ordeal. And as for me, when I feel the urge to pray for one of my children, I get right on it!

"WITH A LITTLE HELP FROM MOM"

JOAN WESTER ANDERSON

Early fall overlooking Virginia's Blue Ridge Mountains . . . could there be a more beautiful season or scene? Sondra Johnson mused as she and her husband, Larry, drove home from a shopping trip in town. It was always nice for the two of them to get away alone together, even if it was simply to do the mundane chores made necessary by their large family. Sondra glanced at her watch. Fourteen-year-old Robert was probably home by now, waiting for them to take him to football practice. And Elsie, Sondra's Holstein, would need to be milked soon. Always lots of things to do on a farm, but Sondra had learned long ago to leave as much as she could in God's hands. "I was brought up praying," she says. "I can never remember when God was *not* a major part of my life."

Less than a mile to go on the curvy road. . . Then, without warning, Larry slammed on the brakes and peered out the windshield. "There's a tree limb blocking the road," he said to Sondra. "But there's something else, too. . . ."

Cautiously they got out of the car. Larry approached the limb to move it aside, then stopped. "Don't come any closer!" he warned Sondra. "It's smoldering—looks like it's been burning."

Burning? Sondra looked around. There were no flames anywhere. Then, even with the shadows obscuring their view, she saw it too: a fallen power line just ahead of the branch, bouncing and shooting sparks!

"I'll run to the Daneks' house and call the power company," Larry decided. "You stay here and wave away any traffic." With any luck, there wouldn't be much, since this road was used mainly by local folks. But if someone were to drive or ride a bicycle into the live power line. . . . Sondra did what came most naturally to her in any situation. She started to pray.

No one had yet come when Larry returned. But Sondra had remembered something in his absence. Robert, waiting for his ride, was going to wonder where his parents were. Maybe they could carefully inch around the downed power line and leave the scene.

No. She went back to the neighbor's house to make another phone call.

"Someone might get hurt if we're not here to warn them," she explained to Robert. "So we won't be able to pick you up for practice until the power company gets here and turns off the electricity."

Robert groaned, "Mom, I can't be late for practice. The coach will make me run laps afterward."

That was true, Sondra knew. Throughout the whole season the coach was particularly rough on boys he thought did not live, eat and breathe football. Robert's self-esteem was a bit shaky too; Sondra would have willingly carried him on her back to practice, if she could, to avoid having him singled out for punishment.

But wait, she realized. Why couldn't Robert come to *them*? She and Larry were less than a mile from their house if Robert took the shortcut through the backfield, which he had done hundreds of times. It meant climbing over the five-strand barbed wire fence separating the Johnsons' property from the Daneks' farm, but Robert was an expert at that, too. "Robert, can I trust you to stay *completely* away from the road and just run to us through our backfields?" she asked. "Dad or I can turn around and take you to practice from here."

"Sure, Mom. I'll be careful."

Sondra hung up, filled with misgivings. Had she done the right thing? Walking back to the car, she prayed intensely. God, please help keep Robert and everyone else safe from danger. Surround us with protection.

No vehicle had yet come down the road, including the electric company truck. The lethal power line continued to quiver like a lightning bolt. And where was Robert? Eight minutes . . . ten minutes . . . Sondra kept eyeing her watch. Robert was a fast runner, he had been ready to leave, and the trip was mostly downhill. What was keeping him? Had he gotten stuck on barbed wire? *God, I place him in Your hands.*

A truck approached. It was the power company. "The electricity is turned off now," the driver announced as he alighted. "Thanks for standing guard."

Sondra barely heard him for, racing down the field toward her, just as she had instructed, was her son.

Relief flooded her. "Oh, Robert, what took you so long?" she cried as he ran to her side.

"It was the barbed wire fence," Robert explained, catching his breath. "I couldn't get over it. It was the strangest thing, Mom. Every time I got close enough to grab on and climb it, I felt pushed back. Like something invisible was in front of me so I couldn't touch the fence. Finally, after a few tries, I just rolled under it."

The power company worker had overheard, and his face turned pale. He walked over to Robert. "It's a good thing you didn't touch that barbed wire, son," he said. "This live power line was lying right across it. You would have been electrocuted."

Under most circumstances, the laws of the universe (and electricity) work in predictable ways. But since God is the Ruler of the world, He can suspend those rules whenever He chooses, to fit His own mysterious plans. Sondra has never doubted that. "But I am still astonished at the things God does," she says today, "not because He can do them, but because He would do them for me."

WHEN THE SMOKE CLEARED

MARIE ANN PELLICANE, AS TOLD TO EVELYN BENCE

Mother loved to tell me about the day Jesus came to my rescue. And I love to tell about the day He came to hers.

The morning started like so many in my childhood. Propped up against fluffy feather pillows, I laid in bed as I had for three years. The only thing that ever seemed to change was the view. Sometimes I looked out my bedroom doorway into the hall at home that led to the large kitchen where my mother brewed aromatic Italian recipes she'd learned in her homeland. Sometimes I stared at the white walls in the children's floor of the Coney Island hospital.

I'd just turned twelve and the doctors were pessimistic about my future. Rheumatic fever had held on too tightly, for too long. My joints were so swollen I couldn't hold a spoon. Even the touch of my bed sheets was painful. Day after day, despite my lack of appetite, Mother coaxed me to eat. Soup, eggs, jellied toast, malts—she'd lift a spoon to my lips and urge me to swallow a bite of life. I, her darling Maria, had to live.

Mother had already lost two children: a baby in Italy, and then her second son in a traffic accident near our home in Brooklyn. When I was six years old, she, my brother Joseph and I were standing on the curb; Joseph wriggled his hand out of

Mother's and darted across the street into the path of a moving van. When an onlooking shopkeeper covered Joseph's crushed head with a butcher's apron, Mother fell into a deep dark well of despair. If her son was dead, she wanted to die too.

In her mourning she tried to take her life. Once I walked into her room just as she finished drinking a bottle of iodine. She lived despite her despair, but I think she never would have climbed out of the dark pit if it hadn't been for three saintly women from Coney Island Christian Church. They came and stayed with us 'round the clock until Mother could again see a ray of hope.

Through the loving witness of those Christian women, Mother came to know Jesus personally. But six years later, when the doctors told her that I would soon die, she grew faint-hearted. She couldn't face the death of a third child, and she told Jesus so, in no uncertain terms. "Lord, if You take away my Maria, I will kill myself. If she dies today, I die too."

She said those words in the kitchen, at the top of the stairway. And five minutes later she saw a stranger—who appeared to be a handsome man with the most beautiful eyes—walking toward her, up the stairs from the main floor. He wore a white robe with a golden cord at the waist. And despite her repeated questions, he said nothing to her. From my room I could hear her talking, "Why didn't you ring the bell? You startled me. Why didn't you knock before you walked in?" Although she was surprised and awed by this stranger's presence in her home, she was amazingly calm and not fearful that he would harm us.

When the man reached the top of the stairs, he kept walking, past the kitchen doorway, past my bedroom and into the living room at the end of the hall. Mother then saw him disappear in a puff that looked like smoke. Mother discerned that her visitor had been Jesus, and two thoughts immediately came to her mind: "Jesus— He's come to heal my Maria . . . or He's come to take her home."

I remember her running into my room. "Maria," she gasped, as if she wanted to make sure I was alive.

Before she said another word, I asked, "Mother, who lifted me up just now?" Although I had seen no one, I'd felt a pair of arms reach under my shoulders and pull me up on my pillows, as my mother often had, as a nurse might.

Immediately my mother realized Jesus had come on a mission of mercy—just when she'd most desperately needed Him. She smiled, and I can still hear her answer. "It was Jesus. It was Jesus."

Then, in her motherly joy, she asked the question she seemed obsessed with: "Would you like something to eat?"

I was surprised at my own answer, "Yes, Mother, I think I would. Could you take me into the kitchen?" At last I was hungry, and that noon, for the first time in three years, I fed myself. As my mother watched and cried, I wrapped my fingers around a spoon and ate a bowl full of her delicious steaming soup.

My bedridden days were over, and within a couple of weeks I was back at school, a member of the real world.

But I was not the only one whose life turned around that day. Before nightfall Mother surrendered herself and dedicated her children, those she had and those yet unborn, to the Lord's service.

For the rest of her sixty-two years she was immovable in her faith. The God of her faith stood by her, even in her old age when her role and mine had reversed. There came a day when I was the one who cooked her meals and spoon-fed her.

Because of diabetes, Mother eventually lost her sight and one leg. Confined to a wheelchair, she moved into the basement apartment of my home in Queens. She was one of us, a part of our small family, the storyteller my grade-school twin boys loved so dearly. She'd been with us for nearly one year when the Lord intervened to save her life. Just when she most needed Him, He again dramatically made known His love and His power.

Mother sat in her favorite spot—pulled up to a long table in her sitting room. There she could reach the dial of her radio, a telephone and her worn Bible which she wanted near even though she could no longer read.

"I'll only be out about forty-five minutes," I told her, "Less than an hour. You know I wouldn't go if it wasn't important." I didn't like to leave Mother alone, but a severe snowstorm had swept down and it still held New York City captive. The roads were impassable to cars. The woman who usually came in to help care for Mother couldn't leave her home. The twins, too young to care for themselves or their grandmother, were at a friend's house playing.

I had to get to the bank, and to do so I'd have to walk three blocks—up two small hills and across 164th Street, the main thoroughfare of Jamaica, Queens—to catch a bus to the business district. I bundled myself up, pulled my fur hat down tightly and, as quickly as the snow allowed, walked out of our residential neighborhood toward the main street.

I wasn't the only one who had to get somewhere, despite the storm. A crowd huddled around the bus stop trying to keep warm. In the group I quickly spotted Antoinette, an older Italian woman who lived in the neighborhood. "How's your mother?" she asked, and we chatted away the minutes. One bus lumbered by, but it was so full the driver didn't even stop and open the doors. We'd have to wait for another—but suddenly the Lord spoke. The command was clear, so compelling that I had no choice but to obey even before I asked any questions. "Go home at once," the Lord said. "Go home. Now. Fast."

Without offering any explanations, I turned my back to Antoinette and darted toward the curb. "The bus," she said. "Aren't you going to wait for the bus?"

I'd startled and confused her but I kept going, simply yelling back over my should, "No, no. I have to go home."

By this time I was asking explanations of God. "Why Lord? Why?" And He immediately gave me an answer: the stove. I'd started to boil some vegetables for Mother's lunch and I hadn't turned them off.

My downhill flight back home was treacherous. I slid. I fell. I ran. And of course I prayed. When I finally caught a glimpse of our brick, columned house, I was slightly relieved. It was still standing, and yet I knew I couldn't slow my pace. The words I'd heard still drove me on, and once I unlocked the front door I was hit with the evidence of the impending disaster: The walls of the house had tightly boxed in a dark cloud of smoke. I flew down the fifteen carpeted steps into Mother's apartment. When I reached the basement kitchen, I didn't even think about my hands. I turned off the burner, picked up the black pot and flung it out the back door into a snow bank which exploded into steam.

I yanked off my scorched leather gloves and heaved them into the yard before turning to Mother, so frightened she hadn't yet realized I was home.

There she sat, right where I'd left her. With her hands raised, she was pleading to her Lord, "Please, please, Jesus, speak to my Maria. Tell her to come home. Jesus, Jesus." In her fear she'd forgotten to dial a telephone operator for help; she'd turned to the One who could respond faster than firemen.

I walked across the thick carpet that had muffled my movements, and I took my mother into my arms. The open doors caused a draft so I wrapped a shawl around her shoulders. Then I sat down on her lap as I had when I was a small child. I stroked her face, as she once had stroked mine. "Mama, I'm here. Everything's okay. Don't worry, Jesus heard your prayers and sent me home."

We cried—tears of alarm, tears of relief, tears of thanksgiving to our God Who again had intervened in our lives.

As I sat and held her I tried to think of something more I could do that would bring my mother the comfort she craved.

Quietly I went into the kitchen and heated a bowl of soup. "Here, Mother," I said when it was steamy hot. Then I lifted a spoonful of life to her lips.

But from everlasting to everlasting
the LORD's love is with those who fear him,
and his righteousness with their children's children—
with those who keep his covenant
and remember to obey his precepts.
The LORD has established his throne in heaven,
and his kingdom rules over all.
Praise the LORD, you his angels,
you mighty ones who do his bidding,
who obey his word.
Praise the LORD, all his heavenly hosts,
you his servants who do his will.
Praise the LORD, all his works
everywhere in his dominion.
Praise the LORD, O my soul.

—Psalm 103:17-22 (NIV)

Accessing God's Power
Participating in Prayer

CHAPTER 5
BEING AN INTERCESSOR

CHAPTER 6
BECOMING AN ANSWER TO PRAYER

Chapter 5   Being an Intercessor

To intercede with God for the needs of others is one of our greatest privileges. To intercede is to present a case, to remind, to advocate for someone who may not be able to plead his or her own cause, and therefore needs the support of others.

Most of us have had the experience of asking for prayer, usually from the spiritual leaders in our lives. We consider intercession to be part of their responsibilities. But often, when we are asked to pray for someone, to intercede with God for a specific need or situation, we panic.

But the truth is that if we leave intercession to the "professionals" or the spiritual giants, we are missing out on one of God's greatest gifts. Intercession is a privilege from God by which we are encouraged to come to Him on behalf of others, lifting us out of ourselves and our own concerns. We become participants in God's work and discover the power and love that He makes accessible to His children. By participating in intercession, a community is created and nourished, where we care for one another and bear one another's burdens. Intercession is not an occasion for fear but an opportunity to unite, both with a loving Father and the people He brings into our lives.

These stories of intercession remind us that what we can't ask for ourselves, someone else can ask for us and God will respond to the prayers of His people.

When we say to people, "I will pray for you," we make a very important commitment. The sad thing is that this remark often remains nothing but a well-meant expression of concern. But when we learn to descend with our mind into our heart, then all those who have become part of our lives are led into the healing presence of God and touched by Him in the very center of our being. We are speaking here about a mystery for which words are inadequate. It is the mystery that the heart, which is the center of our being, is transformed by God into His own heart, a heart large enough to embrace the entire universe. Through prayer we can carry in our heart all human pain and sorrow; all conflicts and agonies; all torture and war; all hunger, loneliness and misery, not because of some great psychological or emotional capacity, but because God's heart has become one with ours.

—Henri J. Nouwen

LETTERS TO A STRANGER

SUSAN MORIN

I t was a bitter January evening in 1992 when the phone rang and my fifteen-year-old son Tajin hollered, "Mom, it's for you!"

"Who is it?" I asked. I was tired. It had been a long day. In fact, it had been a long month. The engine in my car died five days before Christmas, and I had just returned to work after being out with the flu. I was feeling overwhelmed having to purchase another vehicle and having lost a week's pay due to illness. There seemed to be a cloud of despair hanging over my heart.

"It's Bob Thompson*," Tajin answered.

The name didn't register. As I walked over to pick up the phone, the last name seemed vaguely familiar. Thompson . . . Bob Thompson . . . Thompson? Like a computer searching for the right path, my mind finally made the connection. Beverly Thompson. In the brief time it took me to reach the phone, my mind replayed the last nine months.

As I drove to work last March, some patches of snow were still on the ground, but the river, winding on my left, had opened up and was full of swift-moving water. The warm sun coming through my windshield seemed to give hope of an early spring.

---

*Name has been changed.

The winter of 1991 had been a hard one for me as a single working mother. The three children were in their teens, and I was finding it hard to cope both with their changing emotional needs and our financial needs. Each month I struggled to provide the bare necessities.

I faithfully attended church and a Bible study but had very little time for anything else. I longed to serve the Lord in a way that had some significance. So that day I again apologized to Him that I had so little to give back to Him. It seemed I was always asking Him to meet my needs or answer my prayers.

"Lord, what can I do for you? I feel like I'm always taking from you because my needs are so great." The answer to my own question seemed so simple. Prayer.

"Okay, Lord, I will commit this time that I have during my drive to work to prayer. Will you give me some people to pray for? I don't even have to know their needs, just let me know who they are." My heart lifted as I continued to speak to Him during the remainder of my forty-five-minute trip from New Hampshire to Vermont.

I arrived at work and proceeded to open the mail and prepare the deposit. I was in charge of accounts receivable for the Mary Meyer Corporation, a company that makes stuffed animals. I opened one envelope and attached to the check was a note that said, "I'm sorry this payment is late. I have been seriously ill. Thank you, Beverly Thompson."

I can't explain it, but I instantly knew that this was the person the Lord had given me to pray for. "You want me to pray for her, don't you Lord?" I asked him silently. The answer came in a feeling of peace and excitement combined—I knew He had just answered my prayer from less than an hour ago!

So began my journey of prayer for Beverly Thompson. At first I found it very awkward to pray for someone I didn't even know. I did know one thing besides her name. She owned Chapter 1 Bookstore in Presque Isle, Maine, and she ordered bulk quantities of our plush animals to sell. I didn't know how old she was. *Was she married, widowed, single or divorced? What was wrong with her? Was it terminal? Did she have any children?*

The answers to these questions weren't revealed as I prayed for Beverly, but I did find out how much the Lord loved her and that she was not forgotten by Him. Many days I would find myself in tears as I entered into prayer for her. I prayed that He would give her comfort for whatever she would have to endure. Or I pleaded for strength and courage for her to accept things that she might find hard to face.

One morning, as my wipers pushed the spring rain off my windshield, I saw muted tones of browns and greys. I prayed that the Lord would give Beverly eyes to see that that same drab landscape could be transformed into the greens and yellows of spring by a single day filled with sunshine. I prayed she could find hope even though it might seem covered up in the muted tones of her life and rely on a God who can transform winter into spring.

In May, I felt that I should send her a card to let her know I was praying for her. As I made this decision, I knew I was taking a risk. Because I had taken her name from where I worked, I could possibly lose my job. I wasn't in a position to be without any income.

But, God, I told Him, I've grown to love Beverly Thompson. I know You'll take care of me no matter what happens. In my first card, I told Beverly a little bit about myself and how I had asked the Lord for specific people to pray for. Then I mentioned how I had come to get her name. I also told her that the Lord knew all about what she was going through and wanted her to know how much He loved her.

I certainly knew how much God loved me. When I first moved into this new town, it had been difficult, especially as a single mom. But only a few weeks after arriving, I bought a Bible for fifty cents at a yard sale. When I got home, I found a folded note inside.

When I opened it, I couldn't believe my eyes.

"Dear Susan," the handwritten note began, "'he who began a good work in you will carry it on to completion until the day of Christ Jesus' (Philippians 1:6)." Obviously, the writer was encouraging another Susan, since I had randomly picked up the Bible. But for me, it was assurance God was personally interested in me!

Summer came and went and I continued to send Beverly cards and notes. I never heard from her, but I never stopped praying for her, even telling my Tuesday night Bible study group the story. They also upheld her in prayer.

At times I had to admit to God that I really wanted a response; I wanted to know what Beverly thought about this stranger and her steady stream of notes. Did she think I was completely crazy? Did she hope I'd stop?

I took the phone from my son's hand and immediately my hand went clammy. I know why he's calling. He's calling me to tell me to stop bothering his wife. They probably think I'm a religious kook. A million scenarios flew through my mind.

"Hello, Mr. Thompson," my voice squeaked nervously.

"My daughter Susan and I had just been going through my wife's things and found your cards and notes and your phone number. We wanted to call and let you know how much they meant to Beverly and to fill you in on what happened."

My heart loosened as this grieving husband continued to tell me about Beverly's last days.

"While we were going through her things, we found your cards and notes tied up with a red ribbon. I know she must have read them over and over because they looked worn."

Then he said quietly, "My wife had been diagnosed with lung cancer at the age of forty-eight."

I winced at the thought of Beverly's physical setback, but Mr. Thompson's next words comforted me. "She never suffered any pain at all. I know now that this was a result of your prayers."

Then he answered one of the questions I had nagged God about. "The reason you never heard back from her was because she also developed brain cancer," he said.

"Our relationship with God amounted to going to church once in a while, but it was nothing that had much effect on our lives," Mr. Thompson explained. "I wanted you to know that my wife asked to be baptized two weeks before she passed away. The night before she died she told me it was okay for her to die because she was going home to be with her Lord."

As Bob Thompson continued to share his wife's story with me, the drab landscape of my own life was transformed. As insignificant as my life had appeared to be to me, God used it to shine His love upon another life, resulting in a gift that no one could take away.

The experience increased my faith significantly. God took one of the lowest points in my life and added glints of his glory. It made me realize that when we're willing to be obedient, God works in profound ways.

A PRAYER FOR THE SHEPHERD

MIKE NAPPA

Andrae Crouch needed his sleep. It takes a lot of time and energy to be a gospel music singer, pastor of a church, and leader of a street outreach program in urban Los Angeles. And with the recent discovery of three cancerous tumors in his body, Pastor Crouch needed to do all he could do to keep his body healthy.

He was so weary he was tempted not to answer the phone when it woke him at three-thirty in the morning. He was sleeping in the office/apartment attached to Christ Memorial Church, where he pastored, and he wanted to go back to sleep. Still, the call had come in on his private, unlisted line, so he reluctantly reached for the receiver.

"Hello?" he said.

A woman's voice, heavy with a Spanish accent, responded, "Is this the Memorial Church?"

"Yes."

The voice on the phone was firm. "I am to pray for the shepherd."

Andrae was wide awake now. As pastor of Christ Memorial, he was often called the shepherd of his church.

Without hesitation, the woman began to pray, "Father, in the name of Jesus, I pray for the infirmity of this shepherd, and I curse it. I curse it at the root, and it is gone in the name of Jesus."

Then she hung up.

Pastor Crouch lay awake a few moments, wondering how the woman had gotten his phone number, how she knew he had an infirmity, and why she'd called to pray in the wee hours of the morning. He finally returned to sleep.

Two days later Andrae reported to the doctor's office for a checkup. The doctor wanted to assess how quickly the cancer was growing and to begin making recommendations for treatment.

After searching for the tumors for about ten minutes, the doctor put a hand on his hip. "Maybe you can find them, Pastor Crouch, because I don't feel anything."

Andrae pointed and said, "Well, they're here, remember? The big one's right . . . right . . ." Suddenly his eyes filled with tears.

All three of the tumors were gone.

COVERED BY THE CLOUD

SPENCER JANUARY

It was a morning in early March 1945, a clear and sunny day. I was twenty-four-years old and a member of the U.S. Army's 35th Infantry Division, 137th Infantry, Company I. Along with several other companies of American troops, we were making our way through dense woods in the German Rhineland. Our objective was to reach and take the town of Ossenburg, where a factory was producing products that were being used in the war.

For hours we had pressed through an unrelenting thicket. Shortly after midday word was passed that there was a clearing ahead. At last, we thought, the going would be easier. But then we approached a large stone house, behind which huddled a handful of wounded, bleeding soldiers who had tried to cross the clearing and failed.

Before us stretched at least two hundred yards of open ground, bordered on the far side by more thick woods. As the first of us appeared on the edge of the clearing, there was an angry *rat-tat-tat*, and a ferocious volley of bullets sent soil spinning as far as we could see. Three nests of German machine guns, spaced fifty yards apart and protected by the crest of a small hill to the left, were firing at the field. As we got our bearings, it was determined the machine guns were so well placed that our weapons couldn't reach them.

To cross that field meant suicide. Yet we had no choice. The Germans had block-aded every other route into the town. In order to move on and secure a victory, we *had* to move forward.

I slumped against a tree, appalled at the grim situation. I thought of home, of my wife and my five-month-old son. I had kissed him good-bye just after he was born. I thought I might never see my family again, and the possibility was overwhelming.

I dropped to my knees. "God," I pleaded desperately, "You've got to do something. . . . Please *do* something."

Moments later the order was given to advance. Grasping my M-1 rifle, I got to my feet and started forward. After reaching the edge of the clearing, I took a deep breath. But just before I stepped out from cover, I glanced to the left.

I stopped and stared in amazement. A white cloud—a long fluffy white cloud—had appeared out of nowhere. It dropped from over the trees and covered the area. The Germans' line of fire was obscured by the thick foggy mist.

All of us bolted into the clearing and raced for our lives. The only sounds were of combat boots thudding against the soft earth as men dashed into the clearing, scrambling to reach the safety of the other side before the mist lifted. With each step, the woods opposite came closer and closer. I was almost across! My pulse pounding in my ears, I lunged into the thicket and threw myself behind a tree.

I turned and watched as other soldiers following me dove frantically into the woods, some carrying and dragging the wounded. *This has to be God's doing,* I thought. *I'm going to see what happens now.*

The instant the last man reached safety, the cloud vanished! The day was again clear and bright. *I can't believe this.*

The enemy, apparently thinking we were still pinned down behind the stone house on the other side, must have radioed its artillery. Minutes later the building was blown to bits. But our company was safe and we quickly moved on.

We reached Ossenburg and went on to secure more areas for the Allies. But the image of that cloud was never far from my mind. I had seen the sort of smoke screens that were sometimes set off to obscure troop activity in such a situation. That cloud had been different. It had appeared out of nowhere and saved our lives.

Two weeks later, as we were bivouacked in eastern Germany, a letter arrived from my mother back in Dallas. I tore open the envelope eagerly. The letter contained words that sent a shiver down my spine. "You remember Mrs. Tankersly from our church?" my mother wrote.

Who could forget her? I smiled. Everybody called Mrs. Tankersly the prayer warrior. Frankly, I sometimes thought she carried it a bit too far.

"Well," continued my mother, "Mrs. Tankersly telephoned me one morning from the defense plant where she works. She said the Lord had awakened her the night before at one o'clock and told her, 'Spencer January is in serious trouble. Get up *now* and pray for him!'"

My mother went on to explain that Mrs. Tankersly had interceded for me in prayer until six o'clock the next morning, when she had to go to her job. "She told me the last thing she prayed before getting off her knees was this . . ."—here I paused to catch my breath—"'Lord, whatever danger Spencer is in, just cover him with a *cloud!*'"

I sat there for a long time holding the letter in my trembling hands. My mind raced, quickly calculating. Yes, the hours Mrs. Tankersly was praying would have indeed corresponded to the time we were approaching the clearing. And 6:00 A.M.? With a seven hour time difference, her prayer for a cloud would have been uttered at one o'clock—just the time Company I was getting ready to make its daring dash.

From that moment on, I intensified my prayer life. For the past fifty-two years, I have gotten up early every morning to pray for others. I am convinced there is no substitute for the power of prayer and its ability to comfort and sustain others, even those facing the valley of the shadow of death.

PRAYERS FOR ELIJAH

AZRIELA JAFFE

Three hours after giving birth at home to our son, Elijah, I momentarily parted with my sweet baby boy and hobbled down the hallway to my home office. Exhausted and sore from the workout of my life, I mustered the strength to turn on my computer, log on to the Internet, and send an e-mail message announcing Elijah's birth to a group of fifteen hundred people who subscribe to my online newsletter.

To casual observers, I might have looked like another pathetically addicted e-mail junkie, a business owner with priorities so out of whack she couldn't even tear herself away from her home office just hours after giving birth to her child. But they would be wrong.

So why did I even have the desire to share the news of Elijah's birth with my newsletter subscribers? After all, most of them are strangers to me, e-mail addresses from around the world who receive a free online newsletter every two weeks. Writing the newsletter is just one of many tasks in my business. How did this list of strangers, business associates and acquaintances make it to the "A" list: those who heard about Elijah's birth right after calls to our family and close friends? Let me tell you how it happened.

In my third month of pregnancy, my water broke and I almost miscarried Elijah. I was ordered to complete bed rest and warned that I would probably lose the pregnancy. Before retiring to bed, in tears, I sent an e-mail message to my newsletter subscribers explaining the circumstances and asking for prayers from those who believed that prayer would make a difference. Then I went to bed and hoped for the best. Over the next two days, I was inundated with hundreds of prayers e-mailed to me from newsletter subscribers of all faiths, in countries all over the world. My subscribers in turn sent my request for help to their pastors, rabbis, family members and prayer groups, resulting in thousands of prayers for Elijah and me within a twenty-four hour period.

Prayers of all kinds were sent my way. Some quoted Scripture: "When you pass through the waters, I will be with you" (Isaiah 43:2, NIV). And some wove beautiful images for me to focus on: "You and your baby and family are wrapped in love and light." There were prayers from parents who knew what it was like to pray for the life of a child, and prayers from children themselves. This came from a ten-year-old: "Please Lord, help this little baby that Mommy's friend is having and take care of the baby so that we have a new child to love." And one dear soul in Romania wrote, "I don't pray to God too often, but I will pray for you."

Most of the subscribers who responded were strangers to me. We don't normally discuss faith issues in this newsletter—it is, after all, a business newsletter. But I knew that many on the list were devoted and compassionate people, since the focus of the newsletter was taking care of your marriage and family while growing your business. I took a chance by lifting the normal boundaries between business and home and requested help of a personal nature. The result was, I believe, miraculous.

Two days after being flooded with prayers, a neighbor drove me to the doctor's office for my follow-up ultrasound. I held her hand and cried, expecting to hear the worst. Instead, the ultrasound technician was puzzled; he could find nothing wrong. The next day my husband and I visited my medical doctor, who declared me entirely normal. He had no medical explanation for my miraculous recovery. Elijah and I were out of danger, and the pregnancy continued without incident. I will always believe that the thousands of online prayers I received were instrumental in saving Elijah's life.

So when I felt compelled to get the word out to my subscribers only hours after delivering Elijah, it wasn't that I couldn't keep my mind off of my work. It was because these people were now like family to me. I felt as though Elijah had hundreds of aunts and uncles in places as far away as Colombia and Iceland, who loved and cared about him and would celebrate with us his healthy arrival in the world.

RONNIE AND THE PRAYING CHURCH

CHARLIE W. SHEDD

"Vespers" was a service for the young, from babies up to college students. Every Sunday evening at five o'clock they would come. They'd bring their friends, and it was some gathering. Favorite hymns of the children, anthems by the children's choirs, baptisms often. A time for prayer and prayer requests. And "Bible Story Time" instead of "Sermon." Then the moments for questions and answers from the children, for the children. Our bulletin notice read, "Parents are welcome at Vespers, provided they will *not* have anything to say at discussion time. (This notice written by the children.)"

Ronnie was always there with his mother, father and two sisters. Ronnie was five, and this was the year he'd go to kindergarten. It would be a better kindergarten too, because Ronnie was fun, had a big smile and was everybody's friend.

Only this Sunday Ronnie wasn't there. His two sisters, yes, but Walt and Helen, Ronnie's parents, weren't there either. They were at the hospital with a very sick Ronnie. It had come on him all at once and the doctors were puzzled. We had some excellent doctors in our town, and one of their major strengths was that when they didn't know what was wrong, they said so.

This time they'd all said so, and that meant a fast trip to the big city. Almost everybody in our town worked for the same company, and they had a company plane. Executive style, ready to go anywhere on call. But this I thought showed real class: on occasion, when someone was dangerously ill—company worker or not—away the plane would go, carrying one of our citizens.

I talked with Ronnie's mother that Sunday morning, and she said they still didn't know much. All kinds of tests with no diagnosis yet. I prayed with her by phone and assured her we'd be praying for them at all services, including Vespers. And we were.

Ronnie and his family had many friends, all highly concerned. We started this particular Vespers with a simple announcement telling what I knew, followed by a long period of silent prayer. Helen promised she'd call back if there was any change, any news at all.

And there was. At eight thirty that evening I answered our home phone to one of the most jubilant voices I'd ever heard. It was Ronnie's mother.

"You're not going to believe it, but late this afternoon Ronnie sat up, said he was hungry, and asked to go home. When the nurses came they called the doctor. He took one look and asked, 'Whatever happened?' Then he began to examine Ronnie's blood pressure, heartbeat, temperature readings, everything. And the only thing he could figure was that maybe one of the powerful antibiotics finally got through."

Helen paused and then continued. "I told him, 'Doctor, the people in our church were praying for Ronnie today, including the children at Vespers.'"

She laughed, "Do you know what he did then? He turned around, gave me a long look and said, 'Guess the prayers got through too, didn't they? Would you tell them thanks for me?'"

Helen and I talked on for a long time. And then I asked, "Do you remember what time it was when Ronnie sat up and wanted to go home?"

"I certainly do," she answered, "*Wally and I were thinking about all of you praying at Vespers, so we were praying too. That would have been a little after five, wouldn't it?*"

I call on you, O God, for you will answer me;
give ear to me and hear my prayer.
Show the wonder of your great love,
you who save by your right hand
those who take refuge in you from their foes.
Keep me as the apple of your eye;
hide me in the shadow of your wings
from the wicked who assail me,
from my mortal enemies who surround me.

—Psalm 17:6-9 (NIV)

Chapter 6   Becoming an Answer to Prayer

When God answers our prayers, we are awed by His love and concern and humbled by His intervention and personal attention to our needs. Our hearts are filled with gratitude and joy. We bubble over with thanksgiving, excitement and relief. We feel loved and cherished, privileged to receive God's rich blessings, and eager to share His blessing with others.

But consider for a moment those agents of answered prayer, that one person who is in the right place at the right time. She just "happens" to provide a gift of money in the exact amount needed. He just "happens" to find a lost child or feels compelled to retrace his steps to discover a sick woman lying unconscious in the snow. We consider such events coincidence or even "heavenly appointments." Sometimes angels are credited for these remarkable answers to prayer, the quiet rush of their wings whispering in the aftermath.

But more often we find our heroes are simply those who listen to God, those who are sensitive to His voice and leading. These are folks who are responsive, who are willing to cooperate with God. These heroes enter into a partnership with God to accomplish the miracles that He wants to shower on us.

And how do we become agents of the Almighty? That can be answered in one word: obedience. To be willing to act in total accord with God, to respond to His prompting, to be His hands and heart in everyday life.

These stories of God's heroes remind us of our own roles in revealing the hidden hand of God to those around us.

> *"Thy will be done." But a great deal of it is to be done by God's creatures; including me. The petition, then, is not merely that I may patiently suffer God's will but also that I may vigorously do it. I must be an agent as well as a patient. I am asking that I may be enabled to do it. . . . "Thy will be done—by me—now" brings one back to brass tacks.*
>
> —C.S. Lewis

HEAVENLY MISSION

JOAN WESTER ANDERSON

It was November 1990, and Daniel Sheridan was insulating the crawl space in the home he had just purchased. Tomorrow he could finish the job. And since New York City firefighters can swap duty hours with one another, Danny made a few calls and finally got John to work for him the next day.

But late that night, another buddy phoned Danny and asked if John could substitute for *him* instead. Danny protested, but eventually agreed, grumbling all the way.

He was still in a bad mood the next day when he reported for duty. "We started as usual, checking tools, washing the floors—it was pretty uneventful," Danny says. About noon, an alarm sounded on a blaze in an old wooden tenement three blocks from their firehouse. Danny recognized the address and assumed, as the others did, that it was probably one of the many false alarms they received every week.

When a false alarm is suspected, firefighters usually do not put on their heavier coats and helmets. But as Danny got dressed, he was conscious of an inner voice, a distinct prod. "Gear up!" the voice told him. For some reason Danny obeyed.

Danny's truck company was assigned backup position, called Second Due, so the men took their time about pulling out. Yet on the way Danny again felt different, oddly focused on the call. As the siren sounded, his heart raced as if he were being sent on a specific appointment. Was it God? God had always taken care of him, and Danny prayed often. But this intense concentration was unusual. By the time the truck pulled up, Danny had already jumped off.

The tenement *was* burning, with flames shooting through windows on the third floor. The First Due company was on the scene but having trouble opening the hydrant, so Danny raced up the stairs, clogged with firefighters and fleeing tenants, to his assigned position as Forcible Entry Man. "I figured the others would catch up with me in a minute," he says. But because of the initial confusion, his buddies had inadvertently gone into the building next door. Although firefighters should always operate in pairs, Danny was completely alone on the fourth floor.

Rather than put out the fire, a Forcible Entry Man opens a building, starting on the floor above the blaze, and searches for victims. It's a very precarious position because smoke, heat and flames go *up*. But when Danny got to the apartment and opened the steel fire door, he found something unusual. "I was surprised at the lack of smoke," he says, "considering the apartment below was fully involved." Carrying his tools, he crawled into the living room, keeping contact with the wall as a guide. No one was there. Then he worked his way toward the rear bedrooms.

At this point, the fire door on the third floor was opened, and heat and smoke came up the interior stairs and poured into the apartment. Danny inched his way down the hall to the first bedroom. Victims often become trapped in these buildings, but no one seemed to be here.

By now, the apartment felt like the inside of a chimney. Perspiration ran down Danny's face and neck, stinging his eyes. The intense heat reminded him that flames were getting closer, racing up the inside walls. Where were his buddies? Belatedly, Danny realized that it was time to get out before the floor collapsed. Strange, though. . . He still had that sense of heightened awareness, of breath held, of something waiting to happen. Was God trying to reach him?

And then he heard it, just as he turned back. A tiny sound coming from the second bedroom. A cough. A *baby's* cough.

No! Could anyone so small have survived in this temperature? Danny moved toward the sound, feeling his way into the other bedroom, and saw the hazy outline of a crib in the corner. Inside was a newborn infant.

The building residents let out a cheer when Danny staggered out the front door with the ten-day-old baby wrapped in his coat. "We were praying for you—and for him," one woman said before she took little Joel to the hospital.

The baby spent weeks in Intensive Care, but recovered completely. A neighbor had been watching him, but left in panic when the fire started. "I tried to tell Joel's family in the hospital that I think God has big plans for him, because if things didn't happen exactly as they did, he would not be here today," says Danny. "I'm not sure they understood."

But Danny understands why he *had* to work that day, why he suited up completely for an unexpected false alarm, why he seemed propelled onto the fourth floor and strangely reluctant to leave. . . .

There are still dark moments in his life. But then he remembers the day God sent him on a heavenly mission—and the shadows flee.

LOST IN THE NIGHT

RUBEN TIJERINA

I turned up the radio, rolled down the window and merged onto the freeway for the twenty-mile drive home from my job as an armored-car security guard in San Antonio. The cool December breeze felt good on my neck as I glanced out at the dark, swaying trees. After a long day, I was looking forward to getting home to my wife, Valerie, and our three kids.

Checking over my shoulder, I moved into the middle lane. When I turned my head to face forward again, I caught sight of a little girl in a T-shirt and jeans. She was standing on the shoulder of the road, close to the stream of speeding cars. *That's strange,* I thought. Maybe her family had had car trouble, I figured I had passed their car and was already too far down the toad to be much help. *Hope her mom pulls her back a bit.*

I thought again of my own children, eleven-year-old Jeremy, eight-year-old Destiny and two-year-old Victoria. They meant the world to me. But for much of my life, drinking and wild parties had been my number-one priority. I sat through Sunday morning church service—the longest hour of the week—then went out and picked up a six-pack. Just two years earlier I had finally given up drinking and truly committed to God and my family.

I whizzed by a mobile-home park and through an underpass, and checked the dashboard clock. Valerie was probably starting dinner. I missed my family on the job, but after the end of my shift, sometimes my responsibilities at home seemed overwhelming. I wasn't sure I could trust myself to keep up with them when things got tough.

My kids greeted me at the door to our house. I picked up Victoria and made a fuss over Destiny and Jeremy's drawings. After dinner, when I went to tuck in Destiny under her thick cotton blanket, I remembered the little girl I had seen on the freeway. *Hope she's warm in bed too,* I thought, surprised that her image had stayed with me.

In the living room, I sprawled in the recliner and clicked on the TV while Valerie settled down with a magazine on the sofa. I felt myself dozing off when I heard the lead story on the ten o'clock news. "Five-year-old Brittany Key is missing tonight. She is blonde and was last seen wearing jeans and a T-shirt." I jerked my head up. A map of the area being searched flashed across the screen. "Oh, my God," I shouted.

Valerie rushed to my side. "What is it? You're so pale."

"I saw her on the drive home," I said. Though they didn't show a picture of the girl, I was sure it was her. She had been visiting her grandfather's ranch on the outskirts of town when she disappeared that afternoon.

I grabbed the phone and tried to dial the hot line number displayed on the screen, but my hands were shaking so badly I kept messing it up. "Calm down, just calm down," my wife said, taking the receiver from my hands. "Let me call the sheriff."

My wife relayed the location where I had seen the girl. After she hung up, she told me, "They say they've been getting lots of tips. They've got hundreds of volunteers searching."

"But I know exactly where I saw her," I insisted. I had been on that freeway so many times I could find the spot in my sleep. Valerie went to get me a glass of water. I flipped off the TV and sat in silence. *I should have stopped,* I thought. *Why didn't I stop?* I pictured the girl stumbling through the woods, calling for her mommy and daddy. What if she ran into a transient? Or some wild animal? Or ate something poisonous? What if it were one of my kids lost out there? I buried my head in my hands.

Valerie returned and tried to soothe me: "They're bound to find her, honey." I wanted to believe that, but somehow I felt responsible. I had made the wrong decision to drive on. "Do you want to go look for her?" Valerie asked softly.

"Yes," I said.

Quickly, I changed into sweats and we woke the kids. "There's a little girl who's lost. And we're going to help find her," I explained. I went outside to warm the car while Valerie bundled up the children. It had gotten cold enough for me to see my breath. The stars seemed so small in the blackness, not much help to a lost little girl. We piled the kids into the backseat and I headed toward the freeway. Valerie sat quietly beside me, holding a large flashlight.

Please, God, protect that child and guide us to her, I prayed. I clenched the steering wheel so hard my hands ached. *I know You can do great things because You changed my life. Please, Lord, let her be found.* I slowed down as we neared an area where the sky glowed orange from road flares. Police cruisers lined the freeway and barriers blocked our path. The place I had seen the girl was still a good two miles away. "Is this where you're searching for the missing girl?" I asked the officer directing traffic. He nodded.

"But, officer, I saw her farther up the road," I said.

"You're backing up traffic, sir. Move along." He waved us on.

I couldn't believe it. They were looking in the wrong place! I slapped my hand against the dashboard. Then I heard a soft whimpering from the backseat. I looked in the rearview mirror and saw Destiny was crying. "What's wrong, *mija*?" I asked.

"What if nobody can find the little girl, Daddy?"

I sighed. What was I doing dragging my kids out way past their bedtime on this search? Now they were upset too. Maybe I should have left it up to the authorities after all. I pulled the car over and closed my eyes. *"What's the right thing to do, God?"*

I asked. And then I felt His answer, as clearly as if I had actually heard the words: "I will lead you to her. Trust me."

I pulled out my handkerchief and wiped away my daughter's tears. "We're going to find her, don't you worry." It was something I was meant to do, I was sure.

I drove to where I had seen her and slowed to a walking pace on the now-deserted road. My wife shone the flashlight along the edge of the woods. Bugs flew through the beam. Owls hooted from the treetops. We approached the mobile-home park and then the underpass. I caught a flash of white out of the corner of my eye, as fleeting as my glimpse of the little girl earlier.

I backed up and stopped, then flung open the door. I started running up the concrete embankment of the underpass toward what looked like a small white bundle. I slipped, steadied myself, then scrambled on. It *was* her, curled in a ball, a small dog beside her. He raised his head and looked at me with sleepy eyes. I got down on my hands and knees, reached out and touched the girl's arm. She didn't move. My throat tightened. I shook her a bit. "Hey, Brittany," I whispered. Still no response. I shook her again. She stirred, then slowly took a deep breath, and opened her eyes.

"Hi," she said looking at me.

I felt like whooping. "Don't be scared. You're okay now," I said. I scooped her up and ran to the car, the dog following us.

"Daddy, you found her!" Destiny said, her eyes wide. "You found her!"

I wrapped Brittany in a blanket and used my cellular phone to contact the sheriff's department. While we waited for the police to arrive, we asked Brittany how she'd gotten lost. "I was with Papa," she said. "I saw dogs. I called to them and ran and then I couldn't find Papa. I was scared, but Buddy stayed with me." She petted the dog.

Soon helicopters were cruising overhead and the night was filled with whirling lights and screaming sirens. A man pulled up in a pickup truck and jumped out. "Is that my little girl? Is that her?" he asked.

Brittany cried, "Daddy!" I handed her over and Brittany's father hugged her close.

"Thank you so much," he said.

Then I was surrounded by microphones and blinding flashes. "Sir, how does it feel to be a hero?" I heard through the ruckus. Me, a hero? I just went where God directed me.

Today, more than a year later, God still guides me. Not only did I find a lost little girl that night, I found a deeper faith in God, and through Him, in myself.

TRIUMPH IN THE SKY

JOAN WESTER ANDERSON

Dallas Chopping grew up around airplanes. As a two-year-old he sat on his pilot-father's lap, wearing earphones and "flying." While other teenage boys saved for automobiles, young Dallas bought a plane instead. So when he became senior flight captain for a mining company in Casper, Wyoming, he was right where he wanted to be.

In spring 1987, Dallas received an unusual assignment. One of the company's engineers, Michael Stevermer, and his wife, Sandi, had an eight-month-old baby needing a liver transplant. Little Benjamin had been born with biliary atresia, and had already gone through several unsuccessful surgeries designed to buy him some "growing time" until a donor liver could be found. "There are very few infant organs available," Sandi Stevermer explains. "Fifty percent of babies die while waiting for a transplant."

Now a transplant was Benjamin's only remaining chance for life, and he was on waiting lists at hospitals in Omaha and Pittsburgh, places specializing in infant transplants. The Lutheran Brotherhood, a fraternal organization that raises funds for transplants and other needs, had conducted several benefits to cover costs that would be uninsured, and the people of Wyoming had been generous. Everything was in place—except the journey itself. Because the Stevermers lived in such a remote area, it was doubtful they could get an immediate commercial flight to any medical center, especially within the short window of time necessary for surgery to proceed (usually seven to eight hours after a donor organ became available). Nor could the weather be counted upon; when Michael and Sandi had taken Benjamin to Denver for an evaluation a few months earlier, they had almost missed their flight due to heavy snow.

"The Stevermers are wearing pagers now, waiting for a call from one of the hospitals," the company's chief executive officer told Dallas's flight department, "and if one comes, we're authorizing you to use our aircraft—or to do anything else necessary—to get them where they need to go."

Dallas seldom flew east of the Mississippi. But it didn't matter. Surgery would surely take place in Omaha since it was so much closer. However, more than six months passed with no request from the Stevermers. Dallas had almost forgotten about them when, as he worked in his garage late on a fall afternoon, the phone rang.

"There's a liver for Benjamin in Pittsburgh," an emotional Michael Stevermer told him. "Can we get there?"

"I'll meet you at the airport right away." Dallas hung up. Pittsburgh! So much farther than he'd expected, and he didn't have the necessary charts. Maybe the company jet could get them there in time. However, when Dallas phoned his flight scheduler, he discovered that the jet was in use, and the only plane available was a small turboprop. It was not nearly fast enough, and would require a stop for refueling, using up more valuable time.

Worse, the weather forecasts looked ominous. Not only would he be flying into strong head winds, there were thunderstorms over Chicago, and snow predicted for Pittsburgh.

The whole venture was starting to unravel. He couldn't start out on a journey he knew he couldn't finish. Dallas thought of his own two toddlers. How would he feel if *their* lives depended on others?

No, he wouldn't give up before he'd even tried. He frowned, deep in thought. Maybe he could start with the turboprop, and transfer the Stevermers to a faster plane somewhere along the route.

Dallas made a few phone calls from home, trying to locate a charter jet, but he had no luck. He would try again en route. Heading to the airport, he soon lifted Lifeguard 205—with its precious three-passenger cargo—into the sky.

The Stevermers were too absorbed in the immediate situation to realize how concerned Dallas was. "The call from Pittsburgh had actually come in at three-thirty, but I had lost time trying to locate Michael out in the field," Sandi says. "The neighbors had rushed to help me pack and drive me to the airport where I met him. We couldn't give Benjamin anything to eat or drink, and he was cranky before he fell asleep on the plane. I had never met the crew, and I was distracted with everything that had gone on, so I had no idea that we might not make it to Pittsburgh in time." Exhausted, Sandi prayed as she had done from the beginning of her baby's ordeal. "Lord, I can't put Ben through much more. If you're going to take him, do. I put him completely in Your hands." Then she fell into a much-needed sleep.

In the cockpit, however, things were not as calm. "First, the co-pilot and I couldn't find a charter jet for a transfer," Dallas recalls. "Next, Mike mentioned that Pittsburgh had informed him that Benjamin needed to be at the hospital within six hours; otherwise, the liver would go to another child." Six hours! Dallas had not been aware of the time lost trying to locate Michael. It all seemed even more impossible.

Worst of all were the head winds. "Think of them as a moving sidewalk," Dallas explains. "If you're walking at five miles per hour on a moving sidewalk going five miles an hour, you're really covering ten miles an hour. But if you walk in the opposite direction on that sidewalk, you're actually standing still." That was the effect being rendered by the head winds. Although the plane was flying through the air at 240 knots (about 270 miles per hour), the head winds had slowed its progress to 190 knots.

"I had a sick feeling in my stomach," Dallas says, "because I knew I had to tell the Stevermers that it was no use." They had lifted off a little after 5:00 P.M. (7:00 P.M. in Pittsburgh), and thus had less than five hours to complete a journey that, according to his calculations, would take at least seven. There was no way they could do it. Not without a miracle. Dallas put the plane on autopilot, leaned back and closed his eyes. "Father, we need help," he prayed quietly. "This child needs to get to the hospital in time."

Almost immediately, the plane began to shake. Pilot and copilot watched the ground speed indicator in disbelief. It had started to climb. Up, up it went, from 240 to an amazing 340 knots, before the quivering stopped. The silence was broken by the voice of the Denver air traffic controller. "Lifeguard 205, you've really picked up speed. Everything okay?"

"Great!" Dallas answered, still astonished at the wind's sudden—and complete—turnaround. "We have eighty to one hundred knots right on our tail. And everything is smooth."

Pilots of larger aircraft were noticing the phenomenon, too. "What's going on?" they radioed one another. "Things are crazy tonight!" Such sudden, strong wind shifts did occur, Dallas knew, but they were extremely rare. And the chance of him being in the perfect place at the exact moment when they did was even rarer.

But there were still obstacles ahead, especially the cold front expected in Chicago.

When cold air slipped under the warm air, thunderstorms would result, and the little plane would lose precious time detouring around them. Now, as they approached, they could see the front, like a gray wedge lying in the star-studded sky. Yet their radar reported no storm activity. "Father," Dallas murmured again, "You're in charge, and You know what we need."

The front got closer, closer . . . but, unbelievably, as they approached, it had become only a thin mist, wafting gently away into the darkness. No thunderstorms. No lengthy bypass needed after all.

The plane continued its placid journey. Just two hundred miles left until Pittsburgh. By now Dallas should have stopped for refueling. However, the unusual tail wind had pushed the plane along so fast that plenty of fuel remained. They would land at Allegheny County Airport, which was closer to the hospital, rather than the congested Pittsburgh airport, but because of this, new concerns surfaced. "The Allegheny control tower closed at midnight—it was standard procedure," Dallas says. "So there wouldn't be anyone on the ground to tell us where to park and meet the ambulance." Finding it could eat up priceless moments. And was it snowing in Pittsburgh? If visibility was limited, he would need to make a time-consuming instrument approach to the airport or even change airport destinations.

But once again, all the decisions seemed to have been made for them. For Dallas's radio crackled with an updated weather report. Pittsburgh was clear, unrestricted.

There had been no snow, after all. "Oh, and by the way, Lifeguard 205," the controller casually added, "the tower is staying open until you arrive. And your ambulance is standing by at your destination."

Finally the little plane taxied to a stop and its passengers tumbled out, running toward the flickering red lights of the ambulance. "Good-bye, and thanks!" Sandi turned and waved to Dallas.

It was over. "Godspeed," he called. "We'll be praying for you."

Little Ben Stevermer received a new liver in Pittsburgh, and was home and healthy by Christmas. When he was two and a half, and the family had moved to the Midwest, he received an unexpected letter from Dallas Chopping. "I thought I'd wait until you were completely recovered to let you know what a special flight you were on . . ." the letter began.

Only then did Sandi and Michael realize what had taken place. And as Benjamin grows, they plan to tell him more about the night his heavenly Father, some Pittsburgh surgeons and a faith-filled pilot gave him a miracle. They will explain that the plane was too small, the weather too rough, the fuel too limited . . . yet somehow, a seven-hour journey took only four and a half.

For nothing is impossible with God.

"I KNEW YOU WOULD COME"

ELIZABETH KING ENGLISH

Herman and I locked our store and dragged ourselves home to South Caldwell Street. It was 11:00 P.M., Christmas Eve of 1949. We were dog tired.

Ours was one of those big old general appliance stores that sold everything from refrigerators, toasters and record players to bicycles, dollhouses and games. We had sold almost all of our toys; and all of the layaways, except one package, had been picked up.

Usually Herman and I kept the store open until everything had been claimed. We wouldn't have woken up happy on Christmas morning knowing that some child's gift was still on the layaway shelf. But the person who had put a dollar down on that package never returned.

Early Christmas morning our twelve-year-old son, Tom, and Herman and I were out under the tree opening gifts. But I'll tell you, there was something humdrum about this Christmas. Tom was growing up; he had wanted just clothes and games. I missed his childish exuberance of past years.

As soon as breakfast was over, Tom left to visit his friend next door. Herman mumbled, "I'm going back to sleep. There's nothing left to stay up for."

So there I was alone, doing the dishes and feeling let down. It was nearly 9:00 A.M., and sleet mixed with snow cut the air outside. The wind rattled our windows, and I felt grateful for the warmth of the apartment. *Sure glad I don't have to go out on a day like today,* I thought, picking up the wrapping paper and ribbons strewn around the living room.

And then it began. Something I had never experienced before. A strange, persistent urge. It seemed to be telling me to go to the store.

I looked at the icy sidewalk outside. *That's crazy,* I said to myself. I tried dismissing the urge, but it wouldn't leave me alone. In fact, it was getting stronger.

Well, I *wasn't* going to go. I had never gone to the store on Christmas Day in all the ten years we had owned it. No one opened shop on that day. There wasn't any reason to go; I didn't want to, and I wasn't going to.

For an hour I fought that strange feeling. Finally, I couldn't stand it any longer, and I got dressed.

"Herman," I said, feeling silly, "I think I'll walk down to the store."

Herman woke with a start. "Whatever for? What are you going to do there?"

"Oh, I don't know," I replied lamely. "There's not much to do here. I just think I'll wander down."

He argued against it a little, but I told him that I would be back soon. "Well, go on," he grumbled, "but I don't see any reason for it."

I put on my gray wool coat and tam, then my galoshes, red scarf and gloves. Once outside, none of those garments seemed to help. The wind cut right through me and the sleet stung my cheeks. I groped my way down the mile to 117 East Park Avenue, slipping and sliding.

I shivered and tucked my hands inside my pockets to keep them from freezing. I felt ridiculous. I had no business being out in that bitter chill.

There was the store just ahead. In front of it stood two boys, one about nine, and the other six. *What in the world?* I wondered.

"Here she comes!" yelled the older one. He had his arm around the younger. "See, I told you she would come," he said jubilantly.

They were half frozen. The younger one's face was wet with tears, but when he saw me, his eyes opened wide and his sobbing stopped.

"What are you two children doing out here in this freezing rain?" I scolded, hurrying them into the store and turning up the heat. "You should be at home on a day like this!" They were poorly dressed. They had no hats or gloves, and their shoes barely held together. I rubbed their small icy hands and got them up close to the heater.

"We've been waiting for you," replied the older boy. He told me they had been standing outside since 9:00 A.M., the time I normally opened the store.

"Why were you waiting for me?" I asked astonished.

"My little brother Jimmy didn't get any Christmas." He touched Jimmy's shoulder. "We want to buy some skates. That's what he wants. We have these three dollars. See, Miss Lady," he said, pulling the bills from his pocket.

I looked at the money in his hand. I looked at their expectant faces. And then I looked around the store. "I'm sorry," I said, "but we've sold almost everything. We have no—" Then my eye caught sight of the layaway shelf with its lone package.

"Wait a minute," I told the boys. I walked over, picked up the package, unwrapped it and, miracle of miracles, there was a pair of skates!

Jimmy reached for them. *Lord,* I prayed silently, let them be his size.

And miracle added upon miracle, they *were* his size.

When the older boy finished tying the laces on Jimmy's right skate and saw that it fit perfectly, he stood up and presented the dollars to me.

"No, I'm not going to take your money," I told him. I *couldn't* take his money. "I want you to have these skates, and I want you to use your money to get some gloves."

The boys just blinked at first. Then their eyes became like saucers, and their grins stretched wide when they understood I was giving them the skates.

What I saw in Jimmy's eyes was like a blessing. It was pure joy, and it was beautiful. My spirits rose.

After the children had warmed up, I turned down the heater, and we walked out together. As I locked the door, I turned to the older brother and said, "How lucky that I happened to come along when I did. If you had stood there much longer, you would have frozen. But how did you boys know I would come?"

I wasn't prepared for his reply. His gaze was steady, and he answered me softly. "I knew you would come," he said. "I asked Jesus to send you."

The tingles in my spine weren't from the cold, I knew. God had planned this.

As we waved good-bye, I turned home to a brighter Christmas than I had left. Tom brought his friend over to our house. Herman got out of bed; his father, "Papa" English, and sister Ella came by. We had a delicious dinner and a wonderful time.

But the one thing that made that Christmas really joyous was the one thing that makes every Christmas wonderful—Jesus was there.

"GO SEE ROY"

CHARLIE W. SHEDD

The Bible often uses "The hand of God" to reveal God's presence. And because of what I've been through, one of my favorite verses will forever be: "I heard also the noise of the wings. . . . the hand of the LORD was strong upon me" (Ezekiel 3:13–14, KJV).

But one evening I felt more than God's hand. This time I felt the touch of God through my fingers.

It was supper time and I drove into my garage with high anticipation. Always high anticipation for any meal with my favorite cook. Yet this time something else came first.

As I turned off the ignition, my fingers simply wouldn't let go.

"What's going on here?" I asked out loud. From somewhere in my heart came the answer.

Go see Roy. Plain. Clear. No question. From that place in my soul where God and I hold dialogue, I knew He was giving me an order.

"But it's supper time," I argued. I tend to argue with the Lord when I'm hungry.

"Supper can wait, Charlie. Go."

"But why? Roy was in church yesterday. He looked fine."

The only response was silence. So, before another word, I turned on the ignition and went.

Roy was one of our senior citizens. A nice old man, aging too fast but still able to get around, Roy owned several farms, and every day he'd pay a visit to the country. He'd putter about, stand by the fence and admire the calves, the colts, the lambs. He loved his farms.

Roy lived less than a mile north in a big old house, a real landmark. *Hurry Charlie. This could be an emergency.*

And it was.

Dashing up the steps, I found the front door locked. From inside came a moan, but because the curtains were drawn I couldn't see. Hearing the moan again and knowing the quickest route, I rushed to the back door.

The door was unlocked. I rushed to the living room and found Roy on the floor, bleeding, calling for help. Knowing that action was more important than explanation, I checked his cuts and washed the blood away. Then, when I had him clean and quiet, I helped him to the couch.

What happened, he said, was that he'd tripped over a stump behind the corn crib and broke his glasses in the fall.

"But how did you ever drive home, Roy? Six miles, seven? With your face cut and no glasses, however did you do it?"

"I don't know, Charlie. I guess the Lord was with me."

Sometime within the hour, his wife arrived, and she took over. So after hearing his report, the three of us joined hands and had a prayer.

As I turned to go, he said, "Thank you, Charlie. How did you know I needed you?"

I thought I should wait until later to tell him about those stubborn fingers on my car keys. So I answered, "I think it was an angel, Roy."

"Makes sense," he replied. "I was lying there on the floor, praying you would come."

UNSCHEDULED STOP

DALE PAPE

Bringing a railroad train to a halt is no small thing, especially if it's for something you can't explain. On a cold January afternoon in 1997, I was an engineer on our short line, the Adrian & Blissfield Railroad, hauling tank cars back to Adrian, Michigan. Our little line serves agricultural and manufacturing customers in the area. We haul freight to and from the main lines and also run dinner-train excursions on our twenty miles of track.

It was blowing cold that day, so I was glad to be in the warm cab of the 1750-horsepower GP-9 diesel locomotive. I'm general manager of the A & B, but on our railroad I have to be a jack-of-all-trades. I had been running the railroad with three partners and one full-time employee for just six years. That day I was alone.

As I rolled along at about ten miles per hour, something caught my eye. The driveway of a trailer home near the tracks hadn't been plowed. That bothered me. During the summer months I had noticed the yard had always been mowed. Of course, the owner might have gone to Florida for the winter, which a lot of folks around here do. Still, something didn't seem right, although I couldn't put my finger on it.

A thought nagged at me—that I should stop and investigate. I tried to shrug it off. Stopping a train takes valuable time and no small cost in fuel. Besides, I needed to get back to Adrian in time to pick up my wife and attend an event we had both been looking forward to. The restaurant that provides the food service for our dinner train was honoring their employees with a post-holiday party. My wife works part-time in the kitchen on the train. The party was going to be a nice chance to relax a bit after a busy holiday season.

Moreover, there was the "diamond" to think about. That's where our track intersects with the main line. Whichever train reaches the signal first gets to cross it. The other train has to wait, which could be as long as three hours.

That would mean disappointing my wife and missing the party. My wife was expecting our first child. I knew this might be our last evening out for quite a while once our child arrived.

Yet as I rolled along, that thought kept nagging me: *Go back!*

About a quarter mile down the track from the driveway, I closed the throttle and pulled the brake. There was a lot of hissing and groaning as the tank cars clanked and thundered behind me. It took about fifteen minutes to back up to the trailer home. I swung down from the cab and, with the locomotive drumming behind me, trudged through four feet of snow to the house. I felt foolish, expecting to find the place empty or someone at the door wondering why I was bothering him.

Then I saw something. At first I thought it was a kid making a snow angel.

But it wasn't a child. It was an elderly woman lying on her back in the snow, unable to speak. She looked half frozen, her face was red from frostbite. I helped her into the house, then called for an ambulance on my cellular phone. They rushed her to the hospital, where she recovered after several days. She had been lying in the snow for three hours. The paramedics said she wouldn't have lasted fifteen more minutes. I had gotten there just in time.

Mrs. Alice Mae Clough, the seventy-eight-year-old woman who lived alone, had gone out to shovel her walk, fell and couldn't get up. She said, "All I could do was pray for somebody to come along." And who better to come along than the railroad engineer who regularly ran right by her place? I'm thankful I paid attention to that nagging thought to go back.

By the way, my wife and I arrived only a half hour late to the party. It was the best excuse I've ever had for not being on time.

Praise the LORD.
I will extol the LORD with all my heart
in the council of the upright and in the assembly.
Great are the works of the LORD;
they are pondered by all who delight in them.
Glorious and majestic are his deeds,
and his righteousness endures forever.
He has caused his wonders to be remembered;
the LORD is gracious and compassionate.
He provides food for those who fear him;
he remembers his covenant forever.
He has shown his people the power of his works,
giving them the lands of other nations.
The works of his hands are faithful and just;
all his precepts are trustworthy.
They are steadfast for ever and ever,
done in faithfulness and uprightness.
He provided redemption for his people;
he ordained his covenant forever—
holy and awesome is his name.
The fear of the LORD is the beginning of wisdom;
all who follow his precepts have good understanding.
To him belongs eternal praise.

—Psalm 111:1–10 (NIV)

www.guideposts.org
Series Editor: Patricia S. Klein
Designed by Monica Elias
Jacket photo courtesy of Photodisc
Typeset by Composition Technologies, Inc.
Printed in the United States of America

This original Guideposts book was created by the Book and Inspirational Media Division of the company that publishes *Guideposts*, a monthly magazine filled with true stories of people's adventures in faith.

Guideposts is available by subscription. All you have to do is write to Guideposts, 39 Seminary Hill Road, Carmel, New York 10512. When you subscribe, each month you can count on receiving exciting new evidence of God's presence, His guidance and His limitless love for all of us.

Guideposts is also available on the Internet by accessing our home page on the World Wide Web at www.guideposts.org. Send prayer requests to our Monday morning Prayer Fellowship. Read stories from recent issues of our magazines, *Guideposts, Angels on Earth, Guideposts for Kids,* and *Guideposts for Teens,* and follow our popular book of devotionals, *Daily Guideposts.* Excerpts from some of our best-selling books are also available.